S0-AGC-143

MICHAEL JORDAN

**BY PHIL BERGER
WITH JOHN ROLFE**

A SPORTS ILLUSTRATED FOR KIDS BOOK

Copyright © 1990, 1992 by The Time Inc. Magazine Company

All rights reserved. No part of this book may be reproduced in any form or by any electronic or mechanical means, including information storage and retrieval systems, without permission in writing from the publisher, except by a reviewer who may quote brief passages in a review.

Revised Edition
ISBN 0-316-09229-0
Library of Congress Catalog Card Number: 90-50345
Library of Congress Cataloging-in-Publication information is available.

SPORTS ILLUSTRATED FOR KIDS is a trademark of THE TIME INC. MAGAZINE COMPANY.

Sports Illustrated For Kids Books is an imprint of Little, Brown and Company.

10 9 8 7 6 5 4 3 2 1

COM

Published simultaneously in Canada by Little, Brown & Company (Canada) Limited

Printed in the United States of America

Written by Phil Berger with John Rolfe
Cover photograph by John McDonough/*Sports Illustrated*
Comic strip illustrations by Brad Hamann
Interior line art by Jane Davila
Produced by Angel Entertainment, Inc.

For further information regarding this title, write to Little, Brown and Company, 34 Beacon Street, Boston, MA 02108.

Contents

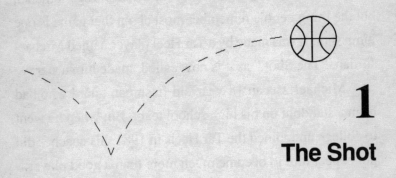

1
The Shot

One of the most exciting games in the history of college basketball was played on the night of March 29, 1982, when the University of North Carolina Tar Heels played the Georgetown University Hoyas. A crowd of 61,612 fans filled the Superdome in New Orleans, Louisiana, to watch the national championship game. It was one of the largest crowds ever to attend a basketball game in the United States, and millions of other people around the country watched on television.

The final score was 63-62. Neither team led by more than six points at any time. The game was not decided until only a few seconds were left on the clock.

There were many great plays and nail-biting moments, but the thing people remember most about that game is one jump shot. It was made by a Tar Heel player named Michael Jordan. "The Shot," as it is now called, made him a star.

Michael was an 18-year-old freshman guard who had been a standout on his high school team. But when he went to college and joined the Tar Heels in 1981, his coaches did not expect him to become much more than a good player.

During 1981-82, Michael scored an average of 13.5 points per game. He was the Tar Heels' third-best scorer. Michael had also been named the Atlantic Coast Conference Rookie of the Year. He had shown flashes of the dazzling talent that has made him the most famous and spectacular player in the NBA today. But he had much to learn, especially about playing defense.

Michael could leap high in the air to make wild, whirling dunks. He could also score on shots from almost anywhere on the court. Yet few people thought of him as the Tar Heels' best player. That honor was given to James Worthy, a forward who was the team's leading scorer. Worthy is now a star with the Los Angeles Lakers. Until the night of that championship game, Michael did not really

2

stand out among his teammates. The biggest reason was that North Carolina's head coach, Dean Smith, insisted that the Tar Heels play together as a *team*. Coach Smith did not like to count on one or two players to score most of the points or make all the big plays. He wanted everyone on the team to contribute. So Michael spent his first year of college ball trying to fit in with his teammates.

Many people expected the 1982 college championship game to be close. The Tar Heels were the Number 1 team in the country. They had won 27 games and had lost only 2 that season before going into the NCAA tournament. The year before that, they had played in the national championship game, but had lost to Indiana, 63-50. Now their opponents were the Georgetown Hoyas [*HOY-yuz*], a team that sportswriters had ranked as the sixth-best college team in the nation.

The Hoyas were actually better than their Number 6 ranking. They had won 26 games and lost 6 that season going into the tournament. Their best player was a seven-foot center named Patrick Ewing, who had been chosen as the Big East Conference Freshman Player of the Year. Ewing was nicknamed "The Hoya Destroya." He weighed more than 200 pounds, and dominated games by using his size to block shots and grab rebounds. Ewing now plays for the New York Knicks and is one of the best players in the NBA.

The Hoyas also had an All-America guard named Eric "Sleepy" Floyd, who had scored more than 2,300 points in four seasons at Georgetown. Floyd now plays with the Houston Rockets.

The Hoyas were a difficult foe for the Tar Heels. They played a tough, physical style of basketball. They were intimidating around the basket as they blocked shots and grabbed rebounds. The Hoyas liked to crowd around an opposing player when he was about to shoot in order to break his concentration. During the 1982 season, their defense was so good that opposing teams had failed to score on more than half the shots they had taken.

The Tar Heels were not as big or as physical as the Hoyas. But they were accurate shooters and they played in a careful, patient way. The Tar Heels liked to pass the ball around until one of them got open for an easy shot. They also used a shrewd strategy called the "Four Corners."

The "Four Corners" was designed by Coach Smith as a way to keep the ball away from other teams and use up the clock whenever the Tar Heels were ahead. When they played the "Four Corners," the Tar Heels formed a box on the court and passed the ball back and forth for as long as possible. Sometimes they passed for more than five minutes. This strategy angered many opposing coaches, players and fans. As a result, the rules of college basketball were changed in 1985 and a shot clock was added in the 1985-86 season. If a shot isn't taken within 45 seconds, the team must give up the ball.

From the opening jump ball, the 1982 college championship game was played with great intensity. The Tar Heels tried hard to score, but each time they shot it seemed that Patrick Ewing was in the way. The Tar Heels got their first eight points only because Ewing was called for goaltending on four shots. (Goaltending is a foul that is called when a player blocks a ball shot by an opponent after the ball begins to drop toward the basket. The team that shot the ball is then awarded two points.)

Eight minutes went by before the Tar Heels scored a basket on their own. And when they started to score, it was only James Worthy who had much success. He scored 16 of his team's first 22 points. But the Tar Heels kept battling and, by halftime, they were behind by only one point, 32-31.

When the second half began, both teams started trading baskets. Up and down the court they ran, with one team scoring and then the other. When the Tar Heels took the lead, 57-56, there were 6 minutes and 4 seconds left to play in the game. Coach Smith told his team to play the "Four Corners."

The strategy almost failed. The Hoyas covered the Tar Heels closely and were often able to get possession of the ball by breaking up North Carolina's passes. The Hoyas stayed within three points of the Tar Heels until there were 3 minutes, 32 seconds left to play. Georgetown scored and North Carolina's lead was cut to one. Then Michael drove hard to the basket and scored to give his team a 61-58 lead.

Georgetown did not give up. Patrick Ewing scored on a jump shot to make the score 61-60. The Tar Heels stuck to their "Four Corners" strategy. It didn't work. With 57 seconds left to play in the game, Sleepy Floyd sank a 12-foot shot to give the Hoyas a 62-61 lead. The Tar Heels tried desperately to score, but the Hoyas covered them so well that North Carolina had to call a timeout to try to change the situation.

The Tar Heels gathered around their coach and planned

one last play. They knew they would have to stick to the smart passing and good shooting that had made them successful.

When play resumed, the final seconds began to tick away. The Tar Heels patiently passed the ball from one to another and hoped someone would get open. That someone was Michael.

With 18 seconds left, Jimmy Black of the Tar Heels saw Michael standing on the left side of the court. Michael was 16 feet away from the basket when he caught Black's pass. He jumped up to shoot. Three Hoyas charged toward Michael to make him take his eyes off the basket. But he just concentrated and took his shot. The ball traveled in a graceful arc . . . right into the basket! The Tar Heels were ahead, 63-62.

The Hoyas then had 15 seconds to tie or win the game. They quickly took off down the court, hoping to catch the Tar Heels before they could set up their defense. Fred Brown of the Hoyas began dribbling the ball in his backcourt. Suddenly, one of the Tar Heels charged at him. Brown then threw a pass toward Sleepy Floyd, who was running down the sideline. Floyd had a clear path to the basket.

Brown did not see James Worthy chasing Floyd until it was too late. Worthy intercepted the pass and tried to dribble out the clock, but he was fouled. He missed both free throws, and Georgetown had one last chance to score. Sleepy Floyd threw up a halfcourt shot at the buzzer that just missed the basket, and North Carolina became the national champion!

The Tar Heels mobbed each other, and their fans flooded out of the Superdome and into the streets of New Orleans to celebrate.

James Worthy was named the Outstanding Player of the Championship Tournament, but Michael returned to North Carolina as a hero. He had made "The Shot."

In Chapel Hill, the town where the University of North Carolina is located, the Four Corners Restaurant named a sandwich made of tongue after Michael because Michael often sticks his tongue out while he's concentrating on the basketball court. (The sandwich has since been changed to roast beef with provolone and grilled onion because tongue sandwiches were not popular.) The local phone company put a picture of his game-winning shot on the cover of its directory. Michael's home town of Wilmington, North

Carolina, honored him with "Michael Jordan Day." When he went out, people came up to him and asked for his autograph.

All that attention began to make Michael feel uncomfortable. "At first I enjoyed the public recognition," he said at the time. "Three years ago, I never dreamed a kid would ask me for an autograph. But, at times, the recognition worries me. When I'm noticed in a restaurant, it's embarrassing. Basketball seems to follow me the whole day."

Michael did not know it then, but basketball would follow him *every* day, for years to come.

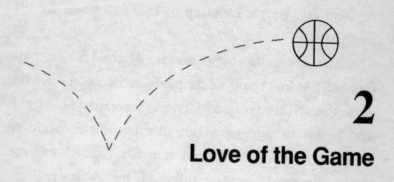

2

Love of the Game

Michael Jordan's famous shot in the 1982 college championship game created a wave of fame and attention. The wave began in North Carolina after the championship game and then began to spread all over the country during the 1982-83 college basketball season.

Michael continued to make great plays and clutch shots in game after game that season. He led the Tar Heels in scoring with an average of 20 points per game. He won All-American honors and was named *The Sporting News* College Basketball Player of the Year.

The next summer, Michael played for the United States national basketball team at the 1983 Pan Am Games in

Caracas, Venezuela. He led the team in scoring and helped them win a gold medal. His coaches raved about him.

George Raveling, one of the U.S. team's assistant coaches, said, "Michael Jordan has the potential to be a truly great basketball player, in a class with Oscar Robertson and Jerry West." Oscar Robertson and Jerry West were two of the greatest guards of all time. Both of them are in the Pro Basketball Hall of Fame.

Fans and sportswriters everywhere now knew how good Michael was. They watched him closely and they wanted to know more about him. They found out that he was humble, friendly and a good student, as well as a terrific basketball player.

Reporter Mike Littwin of *The Los Angeles Times* asked Michael's teammate, Buzz Peterson, what Michael was like. Buzz said, "Michael is a normal kid. He likes to fool around, but he's a real good person."

One day Buzz had to leave the university to visit his aunt, who was sick. When he returned to the apartment that he shared with Michael, Buzz was surprised to see what Michael had done.

"The whole room was cleaned up," he said. "My closet

was fixed, my bed was made and my shoes and sweaters were in the right place. That's the kind of person he is." A considerate person by nature, Michael did it as a favor for Buzz.

People also learned how hard Michael practiced to improve his basketball skills. The day after the Tar Heels won the 1982 championship game, Michael's teammates continued to party and celebrate. Michael went to the gym to practice.

"He improves every month," said Coach Smith. "Look at his defense. When he was a freshman, he had a lot of work to do. Last year he won the 'defensive player of the game' award 12 times. He's going to be one of our great defensive players."

Michael's fame became a tidal wave during his junior season in 1983-84. He won All-American honors and *The Sporting News* College Player of the Year Award for the second time. He led the United States basketball team to a gold medal at the Summer Olympics in Los Angeles, California, in 1984 where people all over the world saw him play.

Michael's career continued to skyrocket after he turned

pro and joined the Chicago Bulls. He has won many awards, including NBA Rookie of the Year in 1985. In 1988, he was the Defensive Player of the Year, MVP of the All-Star Game and the NBA's Most Valuable Player, an award he won again in 1991.

Michael is now the most famous basketball player in the world. Big companies such as Nike, Coca-Cola, Chevrolet, McDonald's and Wilson Sporting Goods have paid him millions of dollars to advertise their products. Fans mob him wherever he goes. They flock to arenas wherever he plays.

Why do people love Michael so much? One reason is the incredible way he plays basketball. Michael can leap so high that he often soars over the basket, which is 10 feet above the court. Great players like Larry Bird of the Boston Celtics and Magic Johnson of the Lakers are as talented as Michael, but no one is as graceful or as colorful. Even people who do not like basketball very much watch him to see what he will do next.

Every time he plays, Michael seems to invent new moves and dunks. Some seem impossible, but he makes them look easy. "He's God disguised as Michael Jordan," Larry Bird once said.

Michael's wizardry on the court has helped create thousands of new basketball fans. During Michael's first season in the NBA, the Bulls sold almost twice as many tickets to their home games than they had the year before. When he plays in other cities, the games are often sold out.

Michael has helped make pro basketball so popular that the NBA has added four new teams to the league since 1988. Those teams are the Minnesota Timberwolves, the Miami Heat, the Orlando Magic and the Charlotte Hornets.

"That's what makes him special," says Kevin Loughery [*LOCK-er-ee*], who was the Bulls' coach during Michael's rookie season. "People come out to watch him and then they find themselves wanting to come back again."

Terry Lyons, a spokesman for the NBA, says, "Listing the guys you go out and pay money to see, Michael's got to be number one. People in Boston might disagree, but when you list all the great players—Larry Bird, Magic Johnson, Dominique Wilkins, Charles Barkley—Michael Jordan is the people's choice."

People find it easy to root for Michael. "Look how we go into hostile places like Boston Garden, and the Celtic fans are cheering for Michael," says Tex Winter, who is an assistant coach with the Bulls. "It's a tribute to his great play and reputation."

Michael is also easy to like as a person. He cares about his family, his friends, his teammates, his fans and people who are less fortunate than he is. Michael visits sick children in hospitals. He holds summer basketball clinics for kids from poor families all over the country. In September 1987, Michael visited a children's hospital in Pittsburgh, Pennsylvania. He brought a basketball hoop into the room and let all the kids shoot baskets from their beds. Then, in January 1990, the Chicago Bulls were in Charlotte for a game against the Hornets. Michael held a basketball clinic for kids the day before the game and then gave away 54 tickets to the kids and their friends. During the Christmas holidays in 1989, Michael was approached by a homeless man who asked for money so he could buy something to eat. Michael gave the man a hundred dollars. "I don't know how it made him feel when I gave him the money, but I know how it made *me* feel," Michael says. "How can anyone experience the warm feeling you get inside when you give something to somebody, and not want to do it again?"

Another year, on Halloween, Michael was unable to be

home to give candy to trick-or-treaters. He left a note on his door asking the kids to come back another day so he could meet them.

In 1987, Michael was given $12,500 as a prize for winning the NBA Slam Dunk Contest. He gave the money to his teammates.

Michael and his wife, Juanita, have two sons: Jeffrey, who was born in December 1988, and Marcus, who was born in December 1990. They live in a large house in a suburb of Chicago. They own a Corvette, a Mercedes and a Porsche. Yet the things Michael enjoys most are simple pleasures like bowling, shooting pool and playing golf. He even has a six-hole putting green in the basement of his house.

No matter how much fame and fortune he has, Michael tries to remain modest. "I don't think those things have changed me," he says. "Money has enabled me to afford the things that I've always wanted. If anything, money and attention have made me wiser about who to trust."

Dave Corzine, who was Michael's teammate on the Bulls from 1984 to 1989, says, "It would have been easy for people to resent Michael with all the points he scores, publicity he gets and money he makes, but nobody does.

Everything is there for him to be a jerk, if he was that way, but he isn't. He just doesn't have that kind of personality. I've never heard him complain about anything. He still works as hard in practice as he does in games."

Practice has made Michael one of the most complete players in basketball history. He is a great offensive player, and one of the best defensive players in the NBA. During the 1987-88 season, Michael became the first player in NBA history to lead the league in both scoring and steals.

Michael's combination of skills is very rare. Only two guards have ever been named to the NBA All-Defensive team during a season in which they led the league in scoring—Jerry West and Michael Jordan.

There are two guards on a basketball team. One is the point guard, who directs his team's offense while he brings the ball upcourt. A point guard must know where his teammates are at all times so he can pass the ball to them when they are open.

The other guard is the shooting guard (also called an off guard). The shooting guard's job is to take shots and help the point guard on defense.

Forwards and centers usually score most of the points

and grab most of the rebounds for a team. Forwards and centers are usually bigger and taller than guards, so it is easier for them to get close to the basket for easy shots. Guards must stay farther back on the court and be ready to play defense in case the other team grabs a rebound and begins a quick attack that is called a fast break.

Michael is a complete guard. He can dribble the ball, pass, rebound, block shots and steal the ball like a point guard. He can also score points with long jump shots like a shooting guard.

Michael is also so good at driving to the basket for dunks and layups that the Bulls allow him to do those things more often than other guards do. In fact, Michael is such an amazing scorer that his career scoring average of 32.6 points per game is the highest in NBA history.

Another reason why Michael is so popular is that he loves basketball. It is easy to see. When he soars to the basket to make one of his rim-rattling dunks, fans can feel his joy. He loves inventing new moves and has won several slam dunk contests. "It's fun and it's what the people want to see," he says. "I'm going to create something people haven't seen yet."

Michael will play basketball any time and anywhere. Few professional teams allow their players to play sports for fun because they might get injured. Michael, however, has a "Love of the Game" clause in his contract with the Bulls that allows him to play basketball in pickup games whenever he wants.

In some ways, Michael is the Peter Pan of basketball. When he's on the court, sometimes it seems that Michael can fly like Peter Pan, too. And when Peter Pan sings, "I won't grow up!"—that's how Michael feels.

"People always ask me how old I am," he told *Sports Illustrated* in 1987, when he was 24 years old. "They think I'm 28 or even 30. I try to project myself as that old. In reality, I never want to grow up."

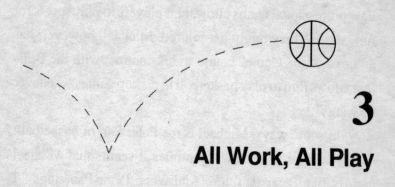

3

All Work, All Play

Everyone must grow up, of course, even Michael Jeffrey Jordan. He did just that in Wilmington, North Carolina. Wilmington is a quiet, seaport town where 48,000 people live. The Jordan family moved there from Brooklyn, New York, shortly after Michael was born on February 17, 1963. Michael is the second youngest of the five Jordan children. He has two older brothers, James and Larry, an older sister named Deloris, and a younger sister, Roslyn. When Michael was younger, his father, James, worked at an electric plant in Wilmington, while his mother, Deloris, worked at a bank.

The Jordan family lived in a two-story brick house on Gordon Street. They were comfortable, but not rich. "I was

16 when I got my first bicycle," Michael says. "I used to get angry that I didn't have one. But we didn't have a lot of money and I think my parents wanted me to appreciate it when I finally got one. I almost slept with that bicycle when I did."

Michael's parents believed that a person could be successful if he worked hard enough. Michael's father started as a mechanic at the electric plant and kept earning promotions until he became a supervisor. His mother started as a teller at the United Carolina Bank and worked her way up to a job as the head of customer service. Mr. and Mrs. Jordan made sure that their children learned to follow their example.

"I was lucky," Michael says. "I have parents who care. They gave me guidance and taught me to work hard. I've learned my lessons."

There was a lot of warmth and love in the Jordan family. That was good for Michael because he was a shy child. He felt funny about himself because his ears stuck out. He was most comfortable when he was at home with his brothers and sisters.

Sometimes Michael and his brothers went out in the yard with their father to fix an old car. But because Michael wasn't very good at working with tools, his dad would send him back inside the house to be with his mother. She taught him to cook and sew instead.

Michael and his parents have always loved and appreciated each other. When he became a star at North Carolina, his mother and father went to every game he played. They even traveled to Hawaii and Greece to watch him.

Michael especially admires his father. In fact, he still imitates him. Mr. Jordan had a habit of sticking his tongue out of the side of his mouth while he repaired car parts on the workbench in the backyard. Today, Michael is famous for the way he sticks his tongue out when he plays.

Coaches have warned Michael that his famous habit is dangerous. He could cut his tongue badly if another player accidentally hits him on the jaw. But at this point, it has become a habit, and habits are hard to break.

Michael and his brothers shared a love of sports with their father. Mr. Jordan had played guard for the basketball team at Charity High School in Rose Hill, North Carolina. "I like to think I was a pretty good player," he says, "but basketball was a seasonal thing then. You'd play for three months and then put the ball away."

Michael and his brother Larry began to play in a local basketball league when they were seven or eight years old. Larry was a good player, and he went on to be a star at Laney High School in Wilmington. Michael, on the other hand, found that his favorite sport was baseball.

Michael played shortstop in Little League. He was also a good pitcher. He says his best childhood memory is of the one-hitter he pitched in the Dixie League championship game when he was 12 years old. "I was the MVP and won a scholarship to the Mickey Owen baseball camp," Michael says.

When Michael entered ninth grade at D.C. Virgo Junior High School, he was a good all-around athlete. He pitched and played outfield in baseball. He played quarterback on the football team and guard in basketball.

Michael was good at basketball, but he was only 5'9" at that time. He knew he would need to grow to play for the varsity basketball team in high school, but that did not seem likely. No one in his family was more than six feet tall.

Even so, Michael still wanted to play varsity basketball like his brother Larry. His brother was also only 5'9", but he could jump high enough to dunk the ball. Michael believed that he could succeed, as Larry had done, by working hard whenever a challenge came his way. He strove to develop his vertical leap in order to compensate for his lack of height. Making the varsity team at Laney High was a challenge, and Michael wanted to prove he could play no matter how tall he was.

Fred Lynch, the basketball coach at D.C. Virgo Junior High, noticed that about Michael. "When I first saw him in junior high, Michael was just average," he says. "Nothing outstanding, really. But the thing about Michael is that he was willing to work hard to become better. He was the first one to practice and the last one to leave. Michael just worked, worked and worked on his game. He played all the time."

When Mr. Jordan saw how serious Michael had become about basketball, he marked off a basketball court in the backyard. He put up a hoop at each end. Michael spent so much time playing and practicing on his new court that the grass was quickly worn away. The dirt underneath became as hard and flat as a wooden floor.

"We played neighborhood games for at least two

hours every day," Michael says. "On Saturdays we were out there all day. Rainy days? We would still be out there. I usually played with guys who were better than me. I always wanted to play with the big boys. It made me a better player, but I didn't know that at the time."

Michael's toughest opponent was Larry. No matter how hard Michael tried, he could not beat his brother in a game of one-on-one.

"Larry used to beat me all the time and I'd get mad," Michael says. "We'd fight all the time. I'd bust his nose or he'd bust mine, and we would be punished for a couple of weeks. He created determination in me."

Even though they fought a lot, Michael admired Larry. The number 23 that Michael has worn on his uniform since high school is a tribute to Larry. Although Larry wore number 45 at Laney, Michael chose 23 because it is approximately one-half of 45. This was Michael's way of saying that he wanted to be at least half as good as Larry.

When Michael entered 10th grade at Laney High, he tried out for the varsity team. Unfortunately, the coaches did not think about how hard he had practiced. They needed tall players, and Michael was then only 5'11". The coaches decided he was too small to play on the varsity team.

So Michael played for the junior varsity team that year. His best friend, Leroy Smith, who was 6'5", played for the varsity.

"I was very disappointed," Michael says. "I averaged 27 or 28 points per game on the junior varsity. When the varsity team went to the state playoffs, I thought I would be called up. When the team went to the regionals, the coach let me on the bus only because a student manager got sick. I didn't have a ticket to get into the game, so I had to carry the uniform of our star player to get in. I didn't want that to happen again. From that day on, I just worked on my basketball skills."

Michael began to work on his basketball skills too much. He cut classes so he could practice and was suspended from school three times. Michael's dad decided it was time for a talk.

"I asked him what his goal was." "He said it was college. I just looked at him and said there was no way he was going. It wasn't going to happen. I was tempted to let it go and hope things got better, but I knew if I didn't do something about it right away it could only get worse."

Michael listened to his father. He understood that if he didn't get good grades in high school, he could not get into a good college.

"I knew he was right and I tried to change," Michael says. "I concentrated more on my schoolwork. I had a goal and I knew I had to work to reach it."

Michael cracked open his books and kept his grades up, but his heart was still on the basketball court. He played in pickup games in a local park whenever he could.

Somehow, Michael also found time to play baseball and football. Sports were an escape for him. He still felt shy about his ears. He felt especially uncomfortable around girls. He says they thought he was "gooney."

"I thought I was never going to get married," Michael says, "so I took home economics courses for three years in high school. I can sew. I can make clothes from patterns, go out and get all the material and stuff like that."

The summer before Michael entered 11th grade, something magical happened. He grew four inches, and was 6'3" tall by the time school opened in September.

"It was almost as if Michael just willed himself taller," his father says.

27

Michael made the varsity team at Laney High that year. He had achieved his goal. But he had a lot of hard work ahead of him.

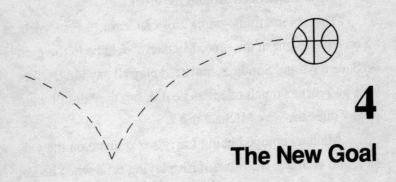

4

The New Goal

When the basketball season began during Michael's junior year at Laney High, he was just another varsity player. His coaches didn't think he was anything special, but they loved how hard he practiced.

"Michael wanted to be the best player he could be," says Fred Lynch, who was the assistant varsity coach at Laney High that year. "He'd go to the junior varsity practice from five o'clock in the afternoon until seven in the evening and go through all their drills and scrimmages. Even the wind sprints. When the junior varsity finished, the varsity team would take over the court and go at it from seven until nine o'clock. Michael would practice again."

Michael practiced around the clock.

"That's something young kids can learn," says Lynch. "You have to put in the time. Michael would be in the gym on Saturdays and Sundays, and he'd play all day long. Other kids had just as much talent as he did, but they didn't want to pay dues the way Michael did."

Michael enjoyed being Larry's teammate on the varsity, and he made the most of his playing time when he got into games. Michael scored baskets with great shots when his team needed them the most.

In the holiday tournament that winter, Laney played its arch rival, New Hanover High School. Michael scored his team's final 15 points and sank a jump shot at the buzzer to win the game.

Michael's performances on the court began to attract attention. There was a school official in Wilmington named Mike Brown who had graduated from the University of North Carolina. Brown was so impressed by Michael that he called Tar Heel Coach Dean Smith to tell him about the fine young player he had seen.

"I think we may have a player here," Brown said. Coach Smith then sent one of his assistants to Laney High to watch

Michael play. The assistant was not completely knocked over by what he saw, but he told Coach Smith that Michael looked like he might be a good college player some day.

Michael was surprised when he found out that he was being scouted by a Division I college like North Carolina. "Division I" is the highest level of college sports, and North Carolina was famous for its basketball teams.

"I never thought I'd be able to play in Division I," Michael says. "Nobody from my high school ever had before."

When Coach Smith later visited Laney High to watch Michael play, Michael sat in a corner dribbling a basketball. He was too shy to speak to the famous coach.

Roy Williams, who was one of Coach Smith's assistants, thought that Michael could become good enough to play Division I basketball if he could test himself against top competition. Williams wrote a letter to the Five-Star Basketball Camp in Pittsburgh, Pennsylvania. He told the camp's director about Michael, and asked him to invite Michael to the camp that summer.

The best high school basketball players in the country attend the Five-Star Camp, but they must be invited first.

They spend three weeks at the camp learning new skills from the top college and high school basketball coaches.

When Michael learned that he had been invited to the camp, he was not sure that he deserved to go. He didn't think he was good enough. He soon found out that he was wrong to feel that way.

During his first week at the Five-Star Camp, Michael won five trophies, including the Most Valuable Player Award. He stole the show from an excellent group of young players. Several of them—Adrian Branch, Ennis Whatley, Anthony Jones and Sam Vincent—would later play in the NBA. Jones and Vincent later became Michael's teammates on the Chicago Bulls.

Coaches and scouts at the camp could not believe what they saw. When Michael soared high above the floor to make a jump shot, one of the scouts said, "It was like there was no defender. He was, like, playing a different game."

The next week, Michael won the MVP Award again and set a camp record by winning five more trophies, bringing his total to 10. He had also proved to himself and everyone else that he was a good player. "That camp changed how I felt about basketball and my future," Michael says. "It was the turning point of my life."

Michael then knew that basketball was his best sport. He had stopped playing football after 10th grade because he had hurt his shoulder. After he attended the Five-Star Camp, Michael decided to quit the baseball team at Laney High, even though several colleges were scouting him.

"I felt I was a better basketball player, but I still think I could have played in the major leagues," Michael says. "Maybe not as a pitcher, but as an infielder or outfielder."

Michael now had a new goal. He wanted a college basketball scholarship. However, he wasn't quite sure about which college he wanted to attend. When he was younger, Michael had rooted for North Carolina State University because his hero, David Thompson, was that school's star player. His mother rooted for the University of North Carolina.

"I hated North Carolina when I was growing up," Michael says. "My mom liked Phil Ford of North Carolina, but I couldn't stand him or any North Carolina guys. I rooted against North Carolina in the 1977 national championship game. My mom got mad at me."

Michael also thought about attending the University

of Virginia. There was a player at Virginia named Ralph Sampson. Many people believed that Sampson was the best college basketball player in the country. Sampson was only a sophomore at the time, so Michael knew that if he went to Virginia, he could play with Sampson for two years.

The news about Michael's brilliant performance at the Five-Star Camp had spread quickly. The University of North Carolina (UNC), North Carolina State and the University of Maryland offered him scholarships. Ironically, Michael chose the school he had hated as a child. He visited the UNC campus and liked what he saw. Not only did North Carolina have a great basketball team and a famous coach, it was also a good place to get an education. And education was impor- tant to Michael. He knew that Coach Smith made sure his players did their schoolwork so they could graduate.

Early during his senior year at Laney High, Michael accepted a scholarship to attend UNC. He had achieved yet another goal, but he continued to practice as hard as ever.

Michael got up early in the morning each day so his head coach at Laney High could drive him to school. He practiced in the gym for an hour before his classes began.

Michael also continued to grow, and was now 6'5". He

scored an average of 27.8 points per game that season and was Laney High's star player. Yet people still wondered if he would be good enough to play for a strong college team like North Carolina. Michael wondered about that, too.

"The people back home, stardom was the last thing they saw for me," he says. "People said I'd go to North Carolina and sit on the bench and never get to play. I kind of believed that myself, but it was a challenge for me."

Michael had no reason to doubt himself. Challenges always bring out the best in him.

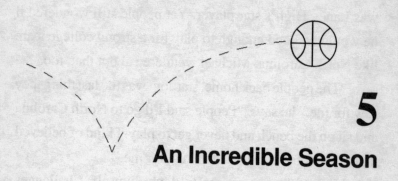

5

An Incredible Season

Michael arrived at the University of North Carolina in September of 1981. He was nervous, and he felt he had to prove himself quickly. His first test was a pickup game in the university's gym with his new teammates.

The competition was tough. Michael had to hold his own against James Worthy, Mitch Kupchak and Al Wood. James was one of the Tar Heels' best players. Mitch and Al were already playing in the NBA.

"Al Wood was guarding me, the score was tied and the team that scored the next basket would win the game," Michael remembers. "I had the ball. I was nervous because people were watching and I wasn't sure I belonged out there.

I went to the baseline and Al went with me. When I made my move, Geoff Crompton came over to help Al. Geoff was nearly seven feet tall. I jumped up with the ball and thought I was trapped, but I just kept going up. I went over both of them and dunked. When I came down to the floor, I said to myself, 'Was that really *me*?'"

Indeed it was. As the days went by and Michael practiced with his teammates, he began to realize that he was just as good as they were. Coach Smith thought so, too. When the 1981-82 college basketball season began, Michael had been named to the Tar Heels' starting lineup.

That was a very special achievement. Coach Smith usually started only sophomores, juniors and seniors because those players had more experience. Coach Smith believed it was better to keep freshman players on the bench so they could watch and learn. Until Michael came along, the only other freshmen that Coach Smith had ever named to the Tar Heels' starting lineup were Phil Ford, Mike O'Koren and James Worthy.

Being chosen as a starter told Michael that Coach Smith believed in him. He also knew that he had to play well or he would be replaced by someone else.

Michael got off to a good start in his first game with the Tar Heels. Playing against Kansas, Michael scored on five of his first 10 shots from the floor and sank both his free throws. In 31 minutes, he scored 12 points. North Carolina won 74-67.

That game made him feel more confident and comfortable. Michael then scored another 12 points against Southern California. He missed only two of his eight shots from the floor. The Tar Heels won again, 73-62.

Michael did even better against Tulsa when the Tar Heels played their first home game of the season at Carmichael Auditorium. He played only 22 minutes, but that was enough time for him to score 22 points, grab five rebounds and get three assists. The Tar Heels won 78-70.

Michael continued to help his team win. The Tar Heels beat South Florida, Rutgers, Kentucky, Penn State, Santa Clara, William and Mary and Maryland. By early January, their record was 10-0. They were the Number 1 team in the nation.

The next game was a big one. It was against Ralph Sampson and Virginia. The game was shown on national television.

Sampson proved to be as good as Michael had heard. He scored 30 points and grabbed 19 rebounds. He played like a one-man team. Michael, James Worthy, Sam Perkins, Matt Doherty and Jimmy Black had to make big plays for the Tar Heels to keep the game close.

In the second half, Michael scored 12 points. With 2:32 left in the game, the Tar Heels led, 57-56. Sampson then faked a 10-foot jump shot, and charged to the basket. He dunked the ball, and Virginia was ahead.

The Tar Heels fought back to take a 61-58 lead with only 15 seconds left in the game. Then Sampson ran to the basket. He waited for his teammates to pass the ball to him while the Tar Heels crowded around him. Even in all that traffic, Sampson was able to get the ball, but his shot missed. The ball bounced off the rim, and Sampson grabbed it. Then he shot and missed again.

This time the Tar Heels got the rebound. They hung on to win, 65-60. North Carolina was still undefeated.

The more Michael played, the more he impressed Coach Smith. "The best thing about Michael is that he pays attention," Coach Smith said at the time. "You tell him something and he does it. He's a freshman with a lot of pressure on him, yet I'd say he's taken no more than two bad shots the entire year."

It was a good time for Michael. He was doing well on the basketball court and in the classroom. He was majoring in geography, and he had a B average. He took his classes seriously. "I know that all those people at the games are here to see me play basketball, not to see me become a better person or get an education," Michael said. "They really don't care about who may give you a job after college, or how you do in life. I don't like to think of things in a bad way, but it can be helpful."

Michael shared an apartment in Chapel Hill with his teammate, Buzz Peterson. Michael had met Buzz at the Five-Star Basketball Camp, and they quickly became best friends. They dated girls together, borrowed each other's clothes and enjoyed a friendly rivalry in golf, pool and cards. It didn't take Buzz long to notice how competitive Michael was.

"There were times," Buzz says, "when Michael made me stay up all night playing cards or pool, refusing to go to sleep until he was winning again."

One night, Michael, Buzz and their dates played

Monopoly. When Michael realized that he could not win, he threw his play money at Buzz and stomped out of the room.

"I stayed with my sister that night," Michael says. "I just couldn't face Buzz."

Michael's burning desire to win helped him the most when he was on the basketball court. He played like an experienced senior and made big plays under pressure. That ability helped the Tar Heels become the national champions that season.

It was a good thing that Michael was able to ignore pressure. He might have flubbed his famous shot if he had thought about the millions of people who were watching him play in the 1982 college championship game.

The Tar Heels' fans were hungry for victory that year because North Carolina had not won a national basketball championship since 1957. Coach Smith wanted to win in a big way. He had been a coach for 21 years and had led the Tar Heels to the national championship game three times, but they had never won.

It is very difficult to win a national championship in college basketball. A team must win enough games during the regular season to be invited to play in the National

Collegiate Athletic Association (NCAA) championship tournament. The winners of the regional divisional tournaments automatically get to go. Only 64 out of the 292 Division I college teams are invited each year. (In 1982, there were only 272 Division I teams.) Those 64 teams are then matched in pairs for the first round. The team that wins the first round game gets to play in the next round. If it loses, it is out of the tournament.

The national tournament lasts three weeks. There are six rounds. Only two teams are left to compete for the championship in the final and sixth round.

All kinds of crazy things can happen during the championship tournament. Good teams can be eliminated by weaker ones when players get cocky and do not play hard enough, or when an opposing player makes a lucky shot at the last second. Making it all the way to the championship game is a rare and special opportunity.

At first, Michael did not fully understand the importance of his game-winning jump shot against Georgetown. "It all happened so fast that it seemed like we had won another game and that was it," he says. "I didn't know how much it meant to people."

Eddie Fogler, the Tar Heels' assistant coach, knew. "That kid has no idea of what he's done," Fogler said, as the Tar Heels whooped it up after the game. "He's a part of history, but he doesn't know it yet."

Michael's father also knew that Michael had done something special. "I knew our lives would never be the same again," said Mr. Jordan. "After that, we weren't private people anymore. We had to adjust to that."

It wasn't long before Michael learned that he would have to make a big adjustment, too. "I couldn't be Michael Jordan anymore," he said. "I became 'Michael-Jordan-who-made-the-game-winning-shot-against-Georgetown.' I didn't want to be remembered only for that. I wanted to be recognized as a complete player."

Michael knew exactly what he had to do to make that happen.

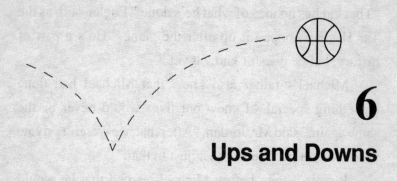

6

Ups and Downs

Before Michael went home for the summer after that championship season, Coach Smith told him to work on his defensive skills, his dribbling and his passing. Michael listened and followed his coach's suggestions.

When Michael returned in the fall of 1982, Coach Smith could tell that he had practiced all summer. He covered opposing players tighter which led to more steals and blocked shots. He had become a more aggressive player.

Michael was named the Tar Heels' "defensive player of the game" 12 times that season. He grabbed an average of 5.5 rebounds per game and was also the team's leading scorer with a 20 points per game average. People began to realize how good Michael had become.

"When Michael hit that shot in New Orleans, he started playing great," said Buzz Peterson. "It exploded his confidence."

Johnny Dawkins, who played guard for the Duke University Blue Devils, said, "Michael goes all out. Not just physically, like he used to. Now he out-thinks you. Of all the players, he's the most impressive."

Tom Newell, now an assistant coach for the Seattle Supersonics, had this to say: "There is one phenomenon in college ball and his name is Michael Jordan."

Bruce Dalrymple, a player on the Georgia Tech team in the 1983-84 season, said, "He's an incredible worker with an incredible amount of talent. That combination makes Jordan so great. His attitude is, 'You can push me or hit me, but I'm going to do what has to be done.' It shows in his face. When Michael gets excited, North Carolina gets going."

As well as Michael played, the Tar Heels were just not as good as they had been the year before. The team missed

James Worthy, who had been drafted by the Lakers. The Tar Heels won 28 games and lost 8, but they were beaten by Georgia in the third round of the championship tournament, 82-77. Michael scored 26 points in that game, but it wasn't enough.

Michael was named *The Sporting News* College Basketball Player of the Year. The award was a great honor, but he did not enjoy it very much. The loss to Georgia hurt. He couldn't wait to begin his next season.

"After my freshman year, when we won the championship, I figured that was the way it was supposed to be," Michael says. "Everybody else was going crazy and I was just acting normal. I didn't know the impact of what we had done, or how special it was. When we lost last spring, I realized how hard I had to work and how hard the team had to work."

Michael spent the summer of 1983 practicing at basketball camps and playing in pickup games. He also helped the United States national basketball team win a gold medal in the Pan Am Games in Caracas, Venezuela. Fame and attention followed Michael wherever he went. He tried not to let those things change him.

"My parents warned me about the traps," Michael says. "The drugs and the drinks, the streets that could catch you if you got careless. I was lazy about some things. I never got into mowing the lawn or doing hard jobs, but I wasn't careless."

Michael learned during his junior year at North Carolina that all the attention and praise *were* affecting him more than he suspected.

After his first four games that season, he found himself in a puzzling slump. His scoring average was only 14 points per game, down from 20 points.

The Tar Heels' fans were also puzzled, but they knew that Michael would play like his old self sooner or later. When Michael scored 19 points against Syracuse, and 25 against Dartmouth, everything seemed to be fine again. But it wasn't.

Michael's ability to score suddenly disappeared again. He scored only 8 points against Iona, 11 points against St. John's and 10 points against Boston University.

Michael's dad thought he knew what was wrong. Mr.

Jordan had been watching Michael play and he told him, "You're trying to force things. You've got enough talent that if you just play like Michael Jordan, things will fall into place."

What his dad said made sense. "I was trying too hard to live up to people's expectations and putting pressure on myself to be as good as they said I was," Michael says. "I was reading too much about myself and paying too much attention to my statistics."

Once Michael relaxed, he began to score, rebound and play great defense again. He exploded in the second half of a game against Louisiana State University (LSU) on January 29, 1984. The Tar Heels were losing at halftime, 37-34, when Michael decided to take over.

First he leaped up to the rim of the basket and caught a pass from his teammate, Kenny Smith, and dunked the ball. Moments later, Michael made a nice pass of his own to Smith, and Smith scored. After that, Michael charged down the sideline to the basket and scored another two points. An LSU player fouled him on that play, so he was given a free throw. Michael made it. Then he scored on another dunk.

In all, Michael scored seven points in less than two minutes. His teammates got fired up, and so did the crowd in Carmichael Auditorium. The Tar Heels went on to win, 90-79. Michael finished the game with a total of 29 points.

"Michael was unreal," said Matt Doherty of Jordan's performance that night.

On February 19, 1984, Michael had another fantastic finish. That one was against the University of Maryland. He scored 19 of his 25 points in the second half of the game, and 13 of these were racked up in the final 10 minutes. He made his best play after his teammate, Steve Hale, had stopped a bad pass from going out of bounds. As he fell forward, Hale threw a pass behind his back. Michael caught the pass at midcourt, drove to the basket, jumped, curled his arm and made a one-handed dunk. Even the Maryland fans cheered.

Sometimes there is a price to be paid for the cheers. When a single player gets too much praise and attention, his teammates can feel jealous. Basketball is a team sport. All five players on the court must work together. It is easy for a player to become angry when he feels he is being slighted.

This did not happen to the Tar Heels. When Michael was on the court, he showed a touch of cockiness that many great players have. Yet, his cockiness was directed at the Tar Heels' opponents. Michael's teammates liked him, and they respected how much he wanted to win.

"When I grew up, I wanted to be able to do anything on the court," says Matt Doherty. "I wanted to grow up to be what Michael grew up to be."

The Tar Heels finished the 1983-84 college basketball regular season with a record of 27 wins and only 2 losses. Michael was the leading scorer in the Atlantic Coast Conference, and he was again named the College Basketball Player of the Year.

North Carolina was expected to do well in the championship tournament. The Tar Heels started fast by beating Temple in the first round 77-66. Michael made 11 of his 15 shots from the floor, and 5 of his 7 free throws, for a total of 27 points.

After that game, North Carolina's fans began to dream about their team playing in the championship game. But to their dismay, the Tar Heels lost to Indiana University in the second round, 72-68. Indiana had a very strong defense that held Michael to only 13 points.

Suddenly, the season was over. So was Michael's career at North Carolina, but the Tar Heels and their fans did not know it at that time.

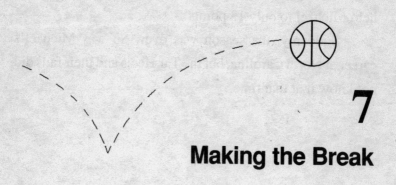

7

Making the Break

Michael had begun to feel restless during his junior year at North Carolina. When he joined the Tar Heels as a freshman in 1981, he had been afraid that he would wind up as a bench warmer. Now he was the team's biggest star. College basketball did not challenge him as much as it once had. He wondered if it was time to test his skills in the NBA.

Michael thought about this for weeks after the Tar Heels lost to Indiana in the championship tournament. Leaving North Carolina was a big decision to make. Most college players do not enter the NBA until after their senior year. Michael was only a junior. Was he really ready to play pro basketball?

Jerry Wachter/Sports Illustrated

North Carolina basketball coach Dean Smith made Michael a starter his freshman year after he saw how good Michael was.

Rich Clarkson/Sports Illustrated

In 1982, Michael's leaps dazzled the crowd at the NCAA semifinal game against Houston at the Superdome in New Orleans, Louisiana.

Manny Millan/Sports Illustrated

Georgetown's "Hoya Destroya," Patrick Ewing, was called for this foul, called goaltending, four times during the NCAA final game against North Carolina in 1982.

Manny Millan/Sports Illustrated

Michael was a man on the move during the NCAA championship game against Georgetown in 1982. North Carolina won 63-62.

Heinz Kluetmeier/Sports Illustrated

Michael, a freshman guard, went up against the Big East Conference Freshman Player of the Year Patrick Ewing in the 1982 NCAA final game. They still compete against each other when the Chicago Bulls (Michael's pro team) play against the New York Knicks (Patrick's pro team).

Rich Clarkson/Sports Illustrated

James Worthy, who was named Outstanding Player of the 1982 NCAA basketball tournament, went on to play for the Los Angeles Lakers. He played on the Lakers 1985, 1987 and 1988 NBA championship teams.

Rich Clarkson/Sports Illustrated

With 18 seconds left in the 1982 NCAA champion-ship game and the Tar Heels down by one point, Jimmy Black (21), the Tar Heels point guard, looked for someone to pass to. That someone was Michael.

Manny Millan/Sports Illustrated

With only 15 seconds left in the 1982 NCAA championship game, Michael made "The Shot" that ended up beating the Hoyas for the title.

Peter Read Miller/Sports Illustrated

Against Spain in the 1984 Olympics in Los Angeles, Michael ran past defenders as if their sneakers had been glued to the floor.

Peter Read Miller/Sports Illustrated

In the gold medal game against Spain in the 1984 Olympics, Michael scored 20 points to lead the United States to a 96-65 victory.

By example, Michael's parents, James (left) and Deloris, showed him that he could be successful if he worked hard enough.

Buck Miller/Sports Illustrated

John McDonough/Sports Illustrated

Michael was an all-around athlete as a kid, and now one of his great loves off the court is golf, which he'd like to play professionally some day.

John McDonough/Sports Illustrated

Michael probably won't be making an appearance in the NFL, but you never know!

The Last 10 Rookies of the Year

1990-91 — Derrick Coleman, New Jersey

1989-90 — David Robinson, San Antonio

1988-89 — Mitch Richmond, Golden State

1987-88 — Mark Jackson, New York

1986-87 — Chuck Person, Indiana

1985-86 — Patrick Ewing, New York

1984-85 — Michael Jordan, Chicago

1983-84 — Ralph Sampson, Houston

1982-83 — Terry Cummings, San Diego

1981-82 — Buck Williams, New Jersey

Bill Smith/Sports Illustrated

Michael was happy to return to playing pro ball on March 15, 1986, after he had broken his foot in the third game of the season. It was almost impossible for him to stay away from the game, even to mend his foot!

Walter Iooss, Jr./Sports Illustrated

Off the court, Michael does a lot of volunteer work with kids who are sick or needy in other ways. In March of 1987, before a game against the Pistons, Michael played wheelchair basketball with a young fan.

The Gatorade Slam-Dunk Championship Winners

1992 — Cedric Ceballos, Phoenix Suns

1991 — Dee Brown, Boston Celtics

1990 — Dominique Wilkins, Atlanta Hawks

1989 — Kenny Walker, New York Knicks

1988 — Michael Jordan, Chicago Bulls

1987 — Michael Jordan, Chicago Bulls

1986 — Spud Webb, Atlanta Hawks

1985 — Dominique Wilkins, Atlanta Hawks

Walter Iooss, Jr./Sports Illustrated

Walter Iooss, Jr./Sports Illustrated

At the 1988 NBA All-Star Game, Larry Bird (above) held the trophy won by the East All-Stars by beating the West All-Stars. Michael (left), was not only the game's Most Valuable Player, he won the Slam Dunk contest with this soaring leap.

John Biever/Sports Illustrated

The Bulls met the Cleveland Cavaliers in the first round of the 1988 playoffs. Chicago won the first two, but then lost Game 3 (above) and Game 4. The Bulls won the fifth, and final, game. The series was important because Michael was helped by his teammates at crucial times.

David Klutho/Sports Illustrated

Even when he's on the bench, Michael shows his competitive fire by urging on other players, as he did in this game against the Charlotte Hornets on February 22, 1989. A month earlier, on the 25th of January, Michael scored his 10,000th point. Michael led the NBA in scoring in the 1989-90 season with a 33.6 points-per-game average and in the 1990-91 season with a 31.5 average.

David Klutho/Sports Illustrated

Michael didn't take many breathers in the 1988-89 season, but he did take at least one (above) in a game against Atlanta in February. During that season, he recorded 15 "triple-doubles" (10 or more points, rebounds and assists in a single game).

Manny Millan/Sports Illustrated

Michael went up for an easy two in a win over the Cavaliers in the 1989 playoffs. The Bulls won the series in five games and they headed for New York and the mighty Knicks in the second round.

Manny Millan/Sports Illustrated

The Bulls met the New York Knicks in the second round of the 1989 playoffs. In the first game (above), Michael jammed for 2 of 34 points and helped lead the Bulls to a 120-109 win in overtime.

Manny Millan/Sports Illustrated

In the overtime period in the first game in the 1989 Eastern Conference Playoffs between the Bulls and the Knicks, Michael soared over Patrick Ewing and Kenny Walker of New York.

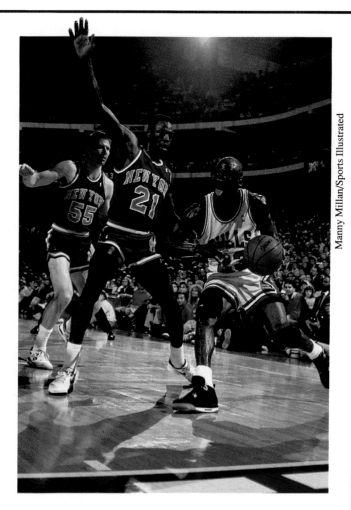

Manny Millan/Sports Illustrated

In Game 3 against the Knicks, Michael scored 40 points, despite being guarded by the likes of Kiki Vandeweghe (55) and Gerald Wilkins (21). Chicago won the game by 23 points, 111-88.

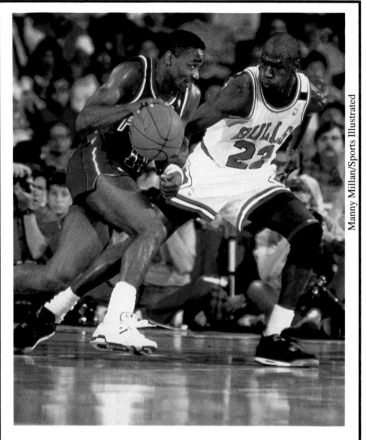

Manny Millan/Sports Illustrated

After the Bulls beat the Knicks in six games, they advanced to the next round—where they met the tough Detroit Pistons. Few people thought the Bulls had a chance of winning even one game, but Michael led his team to two victories before Chicago lost the series. Isiah Thomas (above, left) was Detroit's biggest scoring threat but Michael stayed with him in the first game of the series.

Manny Millan/Sports Illustrated

Michael showed some frustration in the sixth game of the series against Detroit. Even with Michael's 32 points, the Bulls lost the game, 103-94, and the series. The Pistons went on to sweep the Lakers in four games to win the NBA Championship.

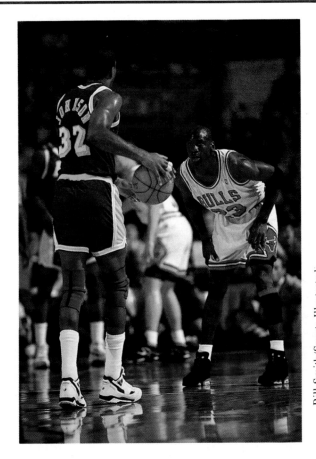

Bill Smith/Sports Illustrated

The '91 championship was billed as a matchup between Michael and Magic. Each player led his team in scoring, assists and minutes played. Magic was denied a sixth championship, while Michael and the Bulls won their first.

Jacqueline Duvoisin/Sports Illustrated

After his basketball career is over, Michael thinks he'll be ready to tackle the professional golf tour. Even though his height works against him in golf and he only gets to practice in the off-season, Michael's handicap is in the excellent 6-to-10 range. Here he carefully studies the green before putting in the St. Jude Classic, which was held on August 2, 1989.

AT LANEY HIGH SCHOOL MICHAEL WAS ALREADY HOOKED ON BASKETBALL, BUT HE WAS ONLY AN AVERAGE PLAYER AND HAD TO WORK HARD TO BECOME BETTER.

MICHAEL'S THE FIRST ONE IN AND THE LAST OUT OF HERE!

HE NEVER STOPS PRACTICING!

GYM

EVEN THOUGH HE PRACTICED ALL THE TIME, MICHAEL DIDN'T MAKE THE VARSITY AS A SOPHOMORE.

WHAT'S MICHAEL DOING HERE? HE'S NOT ON THE TEAM!

IT'S THE PLAYOFF, SO COACH GOT HIM IN BY LETTING HIM CARRY A UNIFORM!

MICHAEL PROMISED HIMSELF THAT THIS WOULD NEVER HAPPEN AGAIN.

BUT HIS DESIRE TO IMPROVE HIS BASKETBALL GAME LED TO SOME BAD CHOICES.

WHERE'S MICHAEL TODAY?

PLAYING BASKETBALL

WELL HE WON'T BE PLAYING FOR LONG IF HE KEEPS CUTTING CLASSES!

WHEN MICHAEL CUT CLASSES FOR THE THIRD TIME, HE HAD GONE TOO FAR AND WAS SUSPENDED FROM SCHOOL.

I'M SORRY SIR!

I HOPE THIS TEACHES YOU A LESSON!

LANEY

LOCKERS

IT WAS MICHAEL'S FATHER WHO PUT MICHAEL BACK ON TRACK. HE TOLD MICHAEL THAT COLLEGE WAS IMPORTANT TO HIS FUTURE...

SO MICHAEL LEARNED TO BALANCE HIS TIME. HE STUDIED AND PRACTICED AND HE LEARNED A LOT FROM HIS BROTHER LARRY.

DID LARRY BEAT MICHAEL AGAIN?

LARRY ALWAYS BEATS MICHAEL ONE ON ONE!

IN A TOURNAMENT GAME AGAINST NEW HANOVER MICHAEL SHOWED WHAT KIND OF PLAYER HE HAD BECOME!

WHAT A CLUTCH SHOT! MICHAEL JUST WON THE GAME FOR US!

AND HE SCORED LANEY'S LAST 15 POINTS! HE'S AWESOME!

BY THE NEXT YEAR MICHAEL MADE THE VARSITY. BUT HE DIDN'T STOP PRACTICING AND WORKING HARD. HE ALSO HAD GROWN FIVE INCHES OVER THE SUMMER HE WAS NOW 6' 3" TALL!

WHAT'S MICHAEL DOING HERE WITH THE J.V.? I THOUGHT HE WAS ON THE VARSITY!

HE IS, BUT HE PRACTICES TWICE A DAY WITH THE J.V. AND THE VARSITY!

Michael knew how important his college degree was, but also he knew that he would do the work necessary to get his degree at a later date, unlike some college players who drop out to join pro teams.

Michael had long talks about this with his parents, Coach Smith and James Worthy. Worthy had left North Carolina before his senior year, and he had quickly become a star with the Lakers. But Michael was aware that many other good college players had failed to make it in the NBA.

That did not seem likely to happen to a player who was as good as Michael. He had enough confidence in himself to think he could succeed as a pro. And he realized that playing another season for the Tar Heels would not improve his game or get him a better NBA contract.

Naturally, the Tar Heels' fans wanted Michael to return for his senior year. But he did not let their feelings influence him. "I don't owe the fans a last year at this university," Michael said. "I have to do what's best for me. If I owe anyone, it's my parents, who have put up with me for 21 years."

On May 5, 1984, Michael announced at a press conference in Chapel Hill that he was leaving the Tar Heels. His decision made headlines in newspapers all over the country.

"Money plays a big part in our lives," Michael said. "Who knows? I may not be around next year. I think it's better to start now. Here is a chance to make a better life for myself and to make me wiser about the life that is going on around me."

The University of North Carolina said farewell to Michael by retiring his uniform number, 23, the following fall. During his three years at the school, Michael had led the Tar Heels to a record of 88 wins and only 13 losses. His jersey now hangs in the Smith Center on the university's campus.

In 1990, Michael honored his school by wearing his blue North Carolina basketball shorts under his Chicago Bulls uniform. He also returned to Chapel Hill for two summers to complete his college degree in geography.

Michael left UNC knowing that he had succeeded in college basketball more than he had ever dreamed he would. His success as a Tar Heel was summed up well by a magazine called the *Blue Ribbon College Basketball Yearbook*. It contained a chapter about the players who would not return to their schools for the 1984-85 season. The yearbook said, "Let's just end this by saying that if Michael Jordan isn't one day considered to be the greatest player in North Carolina history, then the guy who takes that honor in the future must be from another galaxy."

On June 19, 1984, Michael was chosen by the Chicago Bulls in the first round of the NBA college player draft. Michael was the third player to be drafted. Akeem Olajuwon [*a-KEEM o-LYE-je-won*], a center from the University of Houston, was the first player chosen in that draft. He was selected by the Houston Rockets. The Portland Trail Blazers then chose center Sam Bowie of Kentucky.

Michael had a great opportunity that summer to prepare for his rookie season in the NBA. He had been chosen to play for the United States basketball team at the 1984 Olympics in Los Angeles. The coach of that team was Bobby Knight. He was also the coach of the Indiana teams that had beaten the Tar Heels twice in the college championship tournaments. (The Hoosiers of Indiana had beaten the Tar Heels in the championship game the spring before Michael arrived at UNC).

Coach Knight was very demanding. If he did not like the way his players were performing, he told them in the strongest possible language. He didn't care if he hurt anyone's feelings. He was tough to play for, but he had been very successful. Coach Knight had a talent for making good players work hard until they were better. In that way, he was Michael's kind of coach.

"Coach Knight helped me to concentrate and do things without a lot of lollygagging around," Michael said.

Coach Knight made the Olympic basketball players work very hard from April until August. They tested themselves in pickup games against teams of NBA players, where Michael got his first taste of pro competition. Michael learned that even though he had been a hotshot in college, he would have to earn respect in the NBA.

One night in Indianapolis, Michael and his teammates were warming up before a game against some NBA players. One of the balls they were using rolled away to the pro's end of the court. Michael ran after the ball. Before he could get to it, Larry Bird picked it up. Instead of handing the ball to Michael, Bird sneered at him. Then Bird kicked the ball back over Michael's head.

"Bird was showing me it was all business now, and I was beneath him," Michael says. "I didn't forget."

The Olympic Games began in July 1984. Michael and his teammates were ready. Michael scored 14 points against China, 20 points against Canada and 16 points against Uruguay. The United States won all three of those games.

Against Spain, Michael ran past defenders as if their sneakers had been glued to the floor. He sank 12 of his 14 shots and scored 24 points for the game. The United States won 101-68.

After that game, Fernando Martin of the Spanish team was asked what he thought about Michael. Martin said, "Michael Jordan? Jump, jump, jump. Very quick. Very fast. Very, very good. Jump, jump, jump."

Martin's coach said, "Michael's not human. He's a rubber man."

The United States then played Spain, again, for the gold medal. Before the game, Coach Knight walked into his team's dressing room to write the starting lineup on the blackboard. He found a note taped there. It had been written by Michael and it said, "Coach, after everything we've been through, there is no way we're going to lose this game."

Coach Knight put the note in his pocket. Then he walked out to the court and watched Michael keep his promise. Michael scored 20 points as the United States defeated Spain 96-65 and won the gold medal.

Michael's performance in the Olympics showed the world that he was a truly great player. "In two or three years there will be a major controversy in the NBA," said George Raveling, one of the U.S. Olympic team's assistant coaches. "It will be about how Michael Jordan was allowed to be drafted only third instead of first or second."

People still wonder about that fact today. Akeem Olajuwon did become one of the NBA's best centers, but Sam Bowie suffered a series of injuries that kept him from reaching his potential. In the opinion of many, Michael has become the best player in the world.

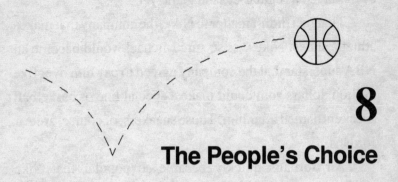

8

The People's Choice

After the Olympics, Michael found out how famous he had become. In October 1984, the Bulls traveled to a high school in Indiana to play an exhibition game against the Milwaukee Bucks. The school's small 6,000-seat gym was packed. A group of teenage girls screamed, "Michael! Michaaael!" as though he were a rock star. They even tried to tear his team jersey off.

"Michael Jackson, eat your heart out," joked Orlando Woolridge, one of Michael's new teammates.

All the craziness around him made Michael quite nervous. "It's the first time I've been through a situation where they were pulling on my clothes," he said. "I mean, I haven't even played a regular-season game yet."

That fact didn't matter to Nike, the company that makes athletic shoes. Nike was so sure Michael would become an NBA superstar that the company agreed to pay him over five million dollars so it could make a special line of basketball sneakers named after him. Those sneakers, of course, are Air Jordans.

Air Jordans quickly became so popular that Nike created an entire series of Air Jordan products, such as tote bags, gym shorts and sweatsuits. Michael's family now manages several stores in North Carolina that sell sporting goods, including Air Jordan products. Michael receives a share of the money from the sale of those products.

After Michael left the University of North Carolina, he had hired a management agency called ProServ. ProServ represents about 200 famous athletes, such as quarterback Boomer Esiason of the Cincinnati Bengals, tennis star Stefan Edberg and bicycling champion Greg LeMond. ProServ helps athletes negotiate good salaries from pro teams and puts together advertising deals like the one Michael received from Nike.

David Falk, who was Michael's agent at ProServ, knew

right away that Michael was very special. Falk told *Sports Illustrated*, "If you were to create a star for the '90s—spectacular talent, midsized, well-spoken, attractive, accessible, old-time values, wholesome, clean, natural, not too Goody Two-shoes, with a little bit of deviltry in him—you'd invent Michael."

The Chicago Bulls knew Michael was special, too. They had agreed to pay him more than six million dollars to play for them for seven years. No guard in the history of the NBA had ever been given so much money.

The Bulls were willing to pay Michael that much money because they desperately needed him. They were one of the worst teams in the NBA at the time, which is how they were able to pick a player so early in the first round of the draft.

The Bulls, who had won only 27 games and had lost 55 the season before they drafted Michael, got the third pick. Not many fans had attended their games and the team was in danger of going out of business. The Bulls' management knew that an exciting star like Michael could bring fans back to their games.

When the Bulls announced that Michael had agreed to

play for them, fans in Chicago began to buy tickets again. The local cable TV station that carried the Bulls' games reported that 30,000 new customers had signed up.

"Michael has certainly lived up to his part already," said Rod Thorn, who was the Bulls' general manager that season. "We were in real trouble here selling tickets, but by drafting him and then having him come off that Olympic showing, it was a shot in the arm for the franchise."

Before Michael left for training camp, he gave his mother a BMW car and his sister a new stereo system.

Michael knew what was expected of him during his first NBA season. He knew expectations would be high. He wanted to prove that he deserved all the money he had been given. He also wanted to be friends with his teammates so they would know that he did not think that he was better than they were.

"I've seen stars isolate themselves," Michael said. "Not me. I like to go to meals with the guys and pick up the tab."

Michael's teammates appreciated his attitude, and they admired how hard he worked in practice. "When he runs and leaps in practice, we all want to try to run and leap with him even if we are tired," said Orlando Woolridge. "I'm so enthusiastic about him that my wife gets tired of hearing me talk about him."

When the 1984-85 NBA season began, Michael did not disappoint his teammates or his fans. He scored 37 points against the Milwaukee Bucks in the Bulls' third game of the season. He scored 45 points against the San Antonio Spurs in the Bulls' ninth game and 25 points or more in 10 of the Bulls' first 15 games.

Michael put on a heart-stopping show nearly every game. Huge crowds went to see him wherever he played.

When the Bulls went to Los Angeles on November 30, 1984, to play the Clippers, a near-record crowd of 14,366 people attended the game. This was a very large turnout for a Clippers game because they were one of the worst teams in the NBA. The size of that crowd was remarkable because the city's other team, the Lakers, was also playing at home. In fact, the Lakers, who were one of the best teams in the league, drew a smaller crowd than usual that night.

Many other NBA teams enjoyed the big crowds that showed up when Michael played in their cities. Harvey Shank, the vice president of marketing for the Phoenix Suns, said, "Michael Jordan coming to town is like having a major entertainer appear in Phoenix. To basketball fans, he is Bruce Springsteen. People line up outside his locker room before warmups just to get a glimpse of him. As soon as he passes by, they go back to their seats."

Fans in every city cheered for Michael as if he played for their team. One night in Oakland, California, he was taken out of a game against the Golden State Warriors so he could rest. The fans began to yell for Bulls coach, Kevin Loughery, to send Michael back into the game. It didn't matter that the Warriors would very likely lose the game if he did. They just wanted to see Michael!

Michael appreciated those cheers. "It gives me a warm feeling," he said. "It started at the Olympics. Even Duke fans cheered for me then." Duke, a university in North Carolina, is one of UNC's biggest rivals.

As the cheers for Michael grew louder that season, some veteran players in the league began to resent him. They didn't like the idea that a young rookie was getting so much praise and attention. Michael found that out when he went to Indianapolis to play in the NBA All-Star Game on February 10, 1985.

The crowd of 43,146 fans in the Hoosier Dome that day

was eager to see Michael test his moves and skills against the league's best players. Michael was a member of the East All-Star Team. He expected to see plenty of action in that game, but he was shocked by what happened.

Michael played for only 22 minutes during the game, and was given the chance to shoot just nine times. The West Team covered him more closely than any other player. When he managed to get open for a shot, his teammates passed the ball to someone else.

After the game, Michael suspected that his All-Star teammates had "frozen him out"—meaning that he had been ignored by his teammates *on purpose.*

Dr. Charles Tucker, a friend of three of the other All-Stars, told reporters that Magic Johnson of the Lakers, Isiah Thomas of the Detroit Pistons and George Gervin of the San Antonio Spurs, felt that Michael was a show-off.

"I met with some of the guys the night before the game and we talked about it," Dr. Tucker said. "The guys weren't happy with Michael's attitude, you know. They decided to teach him a lesson. On defense, Magic and George gave him a hard time and, on offense, the other players just didn't give him the ball."

Isiah Thomas and Magic Johnson denied that this was true. However, Dr. Tucker also told reporters that he had heard players laughing after the game about how they had taught Michael a lesson.

There was a rumor that Michael had angered several All-Stars during the Slam Dunk Contest that had been held the day before the game. During that contest, he had worn gold chains and a warmup suit from his own line of Nike sportswear. The other All-Stars wore regular team warmup gear. They felt that Michael did not show proper team spirit, and that he had tried to call attention to himself.

"That All-Star Game was the most hurting thing in my whole career," Michael says. "I didn't see any reason to be cocky because there was nothing to be cocky about. It was my first All-Star Game and I didn't know what was going on. I wouldn't have worn the Nike warmups if I had known it would cause so much trouble."

When the Bulls played the Pistons shortly after the All-Star Game, Isiah Thomas apologized to Michael. But Michael did not believe that Thomas was sincere. "Mostly show," he said.

But Michael did not get angry. He got even. He scored

49 points that night against the Pistons, as if to say that there was a price to pay for not respecting him.

Whether the other NBA players liked it or not, Michael was truly the people's choice. Few NBA rookies have ever played as well as he did that season. Magic Johnson, for example, scored an average of 18 points per game during his rookie season in 1979-80. Larry Bird scored an average of 21.3 points per game as a rookie that same year. Michael, however, finished his rookie season with a scoring average of 28.2 points per game. He also averaged 5.9 assists and 6.5 rebounds per game.

The only NBA guard who had ever done better as a rookie was Oscar Robertson of the Milwaukee Bucks and Cincinnati Royals. During the 1960-61 season, "The Big O" scored an average of 30.5 points per game. He also averaged 10.1 rebounds and 9.7 assists. Oscar Robertson is now in the Basketball Hall of Fame.

Michael was admired for more than his ability to play basketball. People loved to see how much fun he had when he was on the court.

Curry Kirkpatrick of *Sports Illustrated* wrote, "Michael plays his impassioned game with short-clipped hair, with baggy pants especially tailored an extra two-and-one-half inches long, with vicious rockabye dunks, with that tongue wagging down to his waist as if he were some Pound Puppy in the toy store window."

Unfortunately, the players on other NBA teams did not think it was fun to play against Michael. Michael Cooper of the Los Angeles Lakers said, "There's no way I can stop him. As soon as he touches the ball, the alarm goes off because you don't know what he's going to do. He goes right, left, over you, around and under you. He twists, he turns. And you *know* he's going to get the shot off. You just don't know when and how."

Jerry Reynolds, who is an assistant coach with the Sacramento Kings, said, "If Michael gets 40 points, O.K., you can hold the rest of his team to 65. But you're really afraid he's just going to go nuts. Michael's the only player in the league you can say that about."

The Bulls became a better team because of Michael. They finished the 1984-85 season with a record of 38 wins and 44 losses, and they made the NBA playoffs. Even though they lost three of their four playoff games to the Milwaukee Bucks, the Bulls had proven they could compete against the best teams in the league.

Just as he had done in college, Michael played his best when games were close. He earned a reputation as a game-breaker—he could break the game open for his team. He was the player his teammates looked to during the key moments in games. Players call those moments "crunch time."

It was no surprise when Michael was named the NBA's Rookie of the Year. The award topped off a glorious season and his future looked even better. However, not everything came easily. Michael found that out during his second season in the NBA.

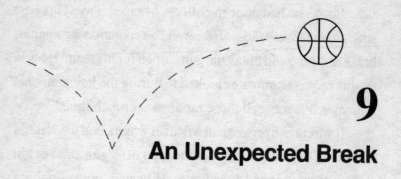

9

An Unexpected Break

When Michael reported to training camp in the fall of 1985, the Bulls had a new head coach named Stan Albeck, who replaced Kevin Loughery. The upcoming season looked promising for the Bulls, and Michael was expected to play even better than he had as a rookie.

All the hope and promise disappeared during the Bulls' third game of the 1985-86 season. Michael broke a bone in his left foot. Doctors told him that he could not play for at least six weeks.

Michael's teammates found out how much they needed him. The Bulls lost eight of their next nine games after he was hurt. Michael sat and watched from the sidelines with a cast on his foot. He was frustrated. He didn't know what to do with himself.

"I've never gone through anything like this before," he said at the time. "I don't know how to deal with it."

Michael did not travel with the Bulls to their road games, or sit on the bench with his teammates when they played at Chicago Stadium. He felt that if he did those things, reporters would concentrate on him and ignore the rest of the team.

"They need their own identity," Michael explained. "If I were with them, I would take a lot of that away."

Michael tried hard to leave the spotlight to his teammates. He spent some time at his home in Northbrook, Illinois. He also visited the University of North Carolina to see his old friends and teammates. While he was there, Michael took a course that he needed to earn his college degree.

"What I learned from this experience is that mentally you have to be tough," Michael said. "At first, the days were going so slow that I found myself just sitting around counting every minute. I had to put my mind to work. I had to keep myself occupied."

Each day that Michael was in Chapel Hill, he did special exercises to help his foot heal. He hoped to return to the Bulls by Christmas, but that did not happen. At the end of December, the doctors gave Michael a new cast. It was lighter than the old cast, and it allowed him to put weight on his foot again. Michael knew it would take a while longer before his leg was strong enough for him to play. "My foot felt a lot lighter when the cast came off," he said. "It's going to take a while for me to get to the form I want. The left leg is my power leg. That's the one I leap off of. I'm not going to push myself, but I'm hoping to be back for the Lakers' game."

That game was to be played on January 20, 1986. When that day arrived, Michael was still unable to play. X-rays showed that the small crack in the bone of his foot had not healed yet. The Bulls' management told Michael to wait until the bone was fully healed.

Michael was very disappointed. He returned to Chapel Hill and secretly played basketball. He knew he was going against his doctor's orders, so he tried to be extra careful.

"I started gradually," he says. "First I took some free throws, then some shots. We got a couple of two-on-two games, then three-on-three. Finally, some of the guys in the gym started a good five-on-five game and I just got involved."

By February, Michael felt that his foot was strong enough to resist another injury. "I couldn't feel anything wrong," he says. "I could tell parts of my game were coming back. When I finally dunked, it felt wonderful." Michael was very careful to land properly after he dunked. He had broken his foot by landing flat-footed, instead of on his toes.

Jerry Krause, the Bulls' general manager, was angry when he found out that Michael had been playing basketball. Michael's doctors had said he could have easily reinjured his foot.

Krause knew how much the Bulls needed Michael. They had lost 43 of their 64 games without him. Fewer fans were attending their home games. As bad as things were, Krause still did not want Michael to come back too quickly. It did not seem likely that the Bulls would make the NBA playoffs that season, so there was no need for Michael to risk another injury.

Michael disagreed. He knew he had been foolish to play at Chapel Hill, but he missed the game he loved so much.

"A lot of people are saying that I'd be a fool to come back," Michael said. "They say I should come back next year. They haven't experienced the game of basketball like I have. I love it like a wife or a girlfriend. I wouldn't do anything to risk my career, but I feel I can play."

Michael returned to the Bulls in March of 1986. He insisted that he was ready to play on the pro level again. "If I had to sit out the rest of the year, I would go crazy!" Michael said.

The Bulls only wanted what was best for Michael, but he missed basketball so much that they could not convince him to rest for another month. Michael told the managers of the team that they could either watch him play games in the NBA, or they could watch him play pickup games in Chapel Hill. No matter what, he was going to play basketball again.

Players often argue with their team's management, and usually the argument is about money. Players often want more money, or a new contract, even though their old contract has not ended yet. Michael argued because he wanted to play. This was unusual.

"How many superstars beg to come back with a broken foot?" asked Coach Albeck. "There are a lot of them who get hangnails and beg to sit out."

The Bulls finally agreed to let Michael play for them again. The owner of the Bulls, Jerry Reinsdorf, told reporters, "The club is not going to stand in Michael's way. Michael was not following doctor's orders when he was in North Carolina. If we knew Michael was going to be good, that's one thing. If he's going to be naughty, I think we're better off letting him play here so at least we can watch over him."

Michael promised that he would stop playing if he felt any pain in his foot. He knew that other players had reinjured themselves by not taking enough time to let their first injury heal.

For example, center Bill Walton was a star with the Portland Trail Blazers when he hurt his foot. He tried to play again too soon and hurt his foot again so severely that it bothered him for more than eight years. After that second injury, Walton never played as well as he once had.

The Bulls did not want Michael to overdo it. They said he could play for no more than six minutes in each half of a game.

Michael returned to action on March 15, 1986, in a

game against the Milwaukee Bucks. A crowd of 15,208 fans filled Chicago Stadium that night.

There were about six minutes left to play in the first half, when Coach Albeck sent Michael into the game for the first time. The crowd stood and cheered. It cheered again when Michael drove up, up, and over Randy Breuer of the Bucks. Breuer is 7'3". Michael sailed over him and jammed the ball through the hoop.

Michael played a little more than 13 minutes that night. He scored 12 points, but the Bulls lost the game, 125-116. Then they lost their next four games in a row. It was clear that Michael could not help the team unless he got more playing time.

Michael tried to make the most of his time in a game. Against the Atlanta Hawks, he stole the ball a total of seven times and set a team record by stealing it five times in one quarter during that game. The best thing was that Michael felt no pain in his foot. The worst thing was that he was so eager to play that he sometimes tried to do too much.

"I was too hyper," Michael says. "But look at it from my point of view: I'm used to pacing myself for a 48-minute game. Now I'm trying to get as much done in seven or eight minutes. I always have one eye on the clock."

The Bulls continued to lose, so Michael asked for more playing time. He was allowed to play for 16 minutes each game, and then 20 minutes.

The more Michael played, the better the Bulls did. They began to win again, and it looked as if they might make the playoffs after all. Eventually, Michael wanted to play for entire games. When the team's management said no, he wondered if the Bulls really cared about winning.

Michael knew that if the Bulls failed to make the playoffs, they could enter the NBA draft lottery. Beginning in 1985, each year the seven worst NBA teams enter a draft lottery. Their names are drawn randomly to decide the order in which they choose eligible college players. Naturally, the team that picks first can draft the best player.

"No one should try to lose to get something better," Michael said. "Just because you don't have a million dollars doesn't mean you go out and rob a bank. A lot of people make do with what they have. Why can't we? Losing games on purpose reflects what type of person you really are."

Jerry Reinsdorf denied that he was holding Michael back so the Bulls could enter the draft lottery. Even so,

Michael was still upset by the strange things that happened to him during games that season.

For example, Michael scored 26 points in a game against the Indiana Pacers on April 3, 1986. When Michael's 28 minutes of playing time ended, he had to sit on the bench even though there were 31 seconds left in the game. Luckily, the Bulls still won, by a score of 109-108.

"If I can play 28 minutes, I think I can play another 31 seconds," Michael said. "I was on a roll at the time. I didn't want to come out. I said to Coach Albeck that 31 seconds can't hurt."

Coach Albeck stuck to the rules. Michael could play for no more than 28 minutes.

George Irvine, the Pacers' coach, did not realize that Michael's time limit had ended. Irvine called a timeout to plan a way to stop Michael from scoring in the final 31 seconds of that game.

"After the game," said Coach Albeck, "he told me he had spent the timeout ordering his players to double and triple-team Michael. You should have seen the look of amazement on Irvine's face when play resumed and Michael was standing on the sidelines with his hands folded."

The Bulls won that game, even though Michael watched from the bench. He still thought the time limit rule was ridiculous and unfair.

"The doctors said that my foot wasn't ready for a full game, but I practice the way that I play," Michael says. "Here I was busting my tail for 90 minutes or two hours in practice. Then I had to beg to play in games."

Coach Albeck felt bad for Michael. "You see him out there doing these amazing things and you are happy to see them," said the coach. "But geez, if something happened to him, it would be an awful, awful thing. Nobody wants to see the end of Michael's career."

Coach Albeck also knew that Michael had given the Bulls a chance to make the playoffs. "There's no way we would be in the position we're in if Michael didn't come back," he said. "He makes everyone play harder."

Michael scored an average of 26.5 points per game during the Bulls' last 10 games that season. They won six of those 10 games, and made the playoffs. The Bulls finished with a record of 30 wins and 52 losses. That was the worst record among the 16 teams that made the NBA playoffs that year.

The Bulls had to play the Boston Celtics in the first round of the playoffs. The Celtics had the best record in the NBA that season. Few people thought that the Bulls had any chance to beat them, even though Michael was told that he could play for as long as he wanted. The Celtics soon discovered what teams had known since Michael was in high school: in big games, Michael Jordan is a special player.

Michael had the ability to "carry" a weak team all by himself. A sportswriter for the *Chicago Tribune* wrote, "Jordan dragged the Bulls to the playoffs, which was the last place they expected or deserved to be."

During the playoff series against the Celtics, Coach Albeck counted on Michael to carry the Bulls once again. He told the Bulls to run plays that were designed to give Michael the ball.

One of those plays was "Number 14." That play called for two Bulls to stay close to the sidelines while two other Bulls stayed under the basket. This left the center of the court open so that Michael could have all the room he needed to make his magic moves.

Michael's job was to keep the ball and go one-on-one against a very good Celtic player named Dennis Johnson.

Johnson was one of the best defensive players in the league. He had been a member of the NBA All-Defensive Team for eight years in a row, including the 1985-86 season. Even so, he was no match for Michael.

In the first playoff game, Michael looked as if he could leap tall buildings in a single bound. He scored on dunks and jump shots. He drove to the basket against Johnson and any other Celtic player who tried to stop him.

Michael scored 30 points in the first half of that game. That total was only three less than the NBA record for the most points scored by a player in one half of a playoff game set by Elgin Baylor of the Los Angeles Lakers in 1962. (This record was broken in 1987 by Sleepy Floyd who scored 39 points in one half against Golden State.) Michael finished that game with 49 points. It was not enough to beat the Celtics, who won 123-104, but it showed Boston how dangerous Michael could be.

"I just sat there and said '*Wow*!'" said K.C. Jones, the Celtics coach. "It was just an awesome performance."

The Celtics players were also impressed. "It would have been fun to sit back and watch," said Robert Parish, the Celtics center. "It was very entertaining for the fans. I have to admit that I was watching a couple of times, myself."

The most amazing thing about Michael's performance that night was that he had not been feeling well. A virus had given him an upset stomach and a headache. He also tired more quickly than usual because he hadn't played very much that season.

"I was pretty tired in the fourth period," Michael said. "I want to win badly, very badly. I want to do things I couldn't do all season. Besides, you know how people are. When you're out of sight, they tend to forget about you. I'm a competitor and I like to be respected as a player."

Michael earned plenty of respect in the second playoff game against the Celtics. He scored on shot after shot. He was sensational when the Bulls ran "clearout" plays. Those plays put Michael's teammates on one side of the court. He then had the other side to himself. As usual, he made spectacular plays at "crunch time."

Michael stole the ball from Robert Parish when there were only nine seconds left to play in the game. The Celtics were leading 116-114. The Bulls then called a timeout and planned a play for Michael.

The play allowed Michael to take a three-point shot. It

would have won the game, but his shot hit the rim of the basket and bounced away. The buzzer sounded and the game appeared to be over. It wasn't. One of the officials had called a pushing foul on Kevin McHale of the Celtics. Michael was then given two free throws.

It was a pressure-packed moment. The crowd of 14,890 in Boston Garden was roaring. They liked Michael, but they wanted their team to win. Michael bounced the ball and studied the basket. Then he calmly sank both shots to tie the score.

The game lasted through two overtime periods. Boston won by a score of 135-131, but the big story was Michael's performance. He had played in 53 of the game's 58 minutes, and had scored a whopping total of 63 points. He had also broken Elgin Baylor's NBA playoff game scoring record that had been set on April 14, 1962.

"I'm really happy for Michael and I've been pulling for him," Baylor said. "He's got all the time in the world, and already he's an amazing player."

Tex Winter, the Bulls assistant coach, said, "I can't remember seeing one player take control of the offense like that in the 50 years I've been associated with basketball.

Michael is the best, most creative one-on-one player I've seen."

Coach Albeck said, "This has to be the greatest individual performance in playoff history. Against the Celtics. In Boston Garden. Against the team that everyone picks to win the NBA Championship. This guy puts on this type of performance. It has to rank way up there."

Michael's performance that night was scary, too—at least for the Celtics. If he could play *that* well even though he had been hurt most of the season, what could he do when he was completely healthy?

After the Celtics eliminated the Bulls from the playoffs, Michael looked forward to answering that question the next season.

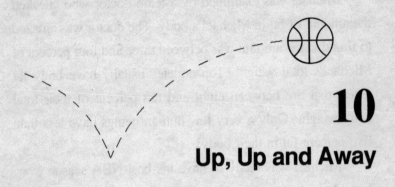

10

Up, Up and Away

The Bulls were eager to have a healthy Michael Jordan in their lineup during the 1986-87 season, so they were very nervous when they learned that Michael had played in an all-star game in Las Vegas, Nevada, that summer.

The Bulls were still afraid that Michael would hurt his foot again. They quietly asked him to rest during the summer. Michael agreed this time.

Instead of playing in pickup games, Michael played 18 holes of golf each day. Golf did not give him as much exercise as a game of full-court basketball, but he was in excellent shape when he reported to training camp in the fall of 1986.

Michael was examined by a team doctor who checked the amount of fat in Michael's body. The doctor was amazed to find that the amount was between three and four percent of Michael's total weight. Top athletes usually have body fat levels that are between eight and ten percent of their total body weight. Only a very few human beings have less than five percent fat in their body!

Michael was ready to have his best NBA season ever. In fact, he became the best scoring guard in the history of the NBA. He led the NBA in scoring with a 37.1 points per game average. He scored 40 or more points in a game 37 times. He scored 50 or more points in a game eight times. He scored 60 or more points in a game twice. He also scored 50 or more points in three games in a row, second only to Wilt Chamberlain, who scored 50 or more points in seven consecutive games—an NBA record. (He also did it in six and five consecutive games on other occasions.)

Wilt Chamberlain was one of the greatest players in the history of the National Basketball Association. He played for teams in Philadelphia and San Francisco from 1959 to 1968, and for the Los Angeles Lakers from 1968 to 1973. He scored 31,419 points during his career and set an NBA record by scoring 100 points in a *single* game against the New York Knicks in 1962.

Michael began the season in New York against the Knicks. A crowd of 19,325 in Madison Square Garden saw him score 50 points. The Bulls were losing, 90-85, in the fourth quarter when they called a timeout. Then they gathered around Doug Collins, who was their new coach, and discussed strategy.

"Coach," Michael said, "I'm not going to let you lose your first game."

Michael then sank one shot after another. He whirled to the basket to dunk. He scored 21 points in the fourth quarter. The Bulls rallied to win 108-103.

Michael's ability to fly into the air and wriggle past defenders amazed everyone who watched him play that night.

"I've never had my leap measured," Michael said. "I was really up there against New York. On my last dunk, I think I was close to eye-level with the rim. Sometimes you just hit your wrists on the rim, but this time it was my elbows and everything."

The Bulls played the Cleveland Cavaliers in their next game. Michael scored 41 points. Then he scored 34 points against the San Antonio Spurs, 33 points against the Detroit Pistons and 39 points against the Phoenix Suns. After five games, Michael had scored an average of 39.4 points per game. Most important, the Bulls had won four of those games.

When the Bulls played at home against the Knicks on November 21, 1986, the "Michael Jordan Air Show" began when there were seven minutes left to play in the game. The Bulls were losing by two points. When Michael floated a 20-foot shot into the basket with one second left in the game, he gave the Bulls an exciting 101-99 victory. He had scored 40 points and set an NBA record by scoring 18 points in a row without missing a shot.

"Eighteen points in a row during crunch time, what else can you say?" asked Hubie Brown, who was the coach of the Knicks.

As always, Michael played his best when he was challenged. Sometimes a challenge would get ugly, as it did when Michael and the Bulls played the Seattle SuperSonics on December 2, 1986.

There were 34 seconds left in that game when Michael scored on a three-point play to tie the score. The game then went into overtime and he scored the Bulls' first eight points. When he drove to the basket to dunk, he was fouled by Xavier [*ZAY-vee-er*] McDaniel of the Sonics.

Michael stepped to the foul line to take his free throws. Then the trouble started. Michael and McDaniel exchanged harsh words. McDaniel, who is 6'7", pointed his finger in Michael's face. Michael pointed back.

"He tapped me in my face and I let it go by," Michael says. "I think he was trying to intimidate me."

It didn't work. Michael scored on both free throws to give the Bulls a 111-109 lead. Then the Sonics called a timeout. When they put the ball back in play, Michael blocked a shot by Tom Chambers of the Sonics. It was Michael's sixth blocked shot of the game.

The Bulls grabbed the ball and ran downcourt. Michael caught a pass, and his eyes lit up. He drove right at McDaniel, faked him off his feet, and scored on a 17-foot jump shot. As he turned to go back upcourt, Michael stared at McDaniel. There was nothing McDaniel could say. The Bulls went on to win, 115-109. Michael had scored a total of 40 points.

"I dug down for that extra ten percent," Michael said

after the game. "I knew McDaniel was going to be pumped up. When I faked, I knew he was going to go for it."

Coach Collins was happy that McDaniel had made Michael angry. "When Michael got that look in his eyes, I knew the game was over," he said. "He would never be denied after that."

Michael was unstoppable night after night. On April 13, 1987, he scored 50 points against the Milwaukee Bucks. Don Nelson, the Bucks coach, then whipped off his necktie. Nelson wrote on it, "Great Season, Great Person," and gave the tie to Michael.

Three nights later, against the Atlanta Hawks, Michael set another NBA record when he scored 23 points in a row without missing a shot. He also scored a total of 61 points in that game. As the game ended, Michael took one last shot from midcourt, but it fell just short of the basket.

"Michael was an inch exhausted," joked Doc Rivers of the Hawks.

Michael did more than score points that season. He took pride in being a complete player, and he worked hard on his defense. He became the first player in NBA history to have more than 200 steals and 100 blocks in the same season.

"When he concentrates on it, he's a totally great defensive player, as good as there is in this league," said Jerry Reynolds, an assistant coach of the Sacramento Kings. "If he only had to score 15 or 16 points a game, he would be *the* best on defense."

When Michael was asked about the best game he had played that season, he picked the night of March 4, 1987, against the Detroit Pistons. "I switched onto Adrian Dantley in the last few minutes, stole the ball three times and held him without a basket," Michael said. "A victory for defense." What Michael forgot to mention was that along with his superb defense, he scored a whopping 61 points!

Michael finished the season as the first NBA player since Wilt Chamberlain (in 1962-63) to score more than 3,000 points in one year. The Bulls made the NBA playoffs with a record of 40 wins and 42 losses. Unfortunately, they were defeated again by the Celtics in three games. Michael averaged 35.6 points, 7 rebounds, 6 assists, 2 steals, and 2.3 blocks per game in that playoff series. He had done his best, but it wasn't enough.

It was clear that the Bulls would not be able to beat good teams in the playoffs if they kept counting on Michael alone to carry them. Charles Oakley and John Paxson were the only other Bulls who had scoring averages of more than nine points per game that season. Other teams knew that they could not completely stop Michael, so they tried to hold him to as few points as possible.

"I'm disappointed when my teammates don't play as well as I expect them to," Michael says. "They have a tendency to stand around and let me do everything. I get disappointed that they aren't respected, yet they don't respond."

The loss to the Celtics in the playoffs hurt. Michael wanted to win an NBA championship very much. Even though he was a great player, he would need help before he and the Bulls could achieve that goal.

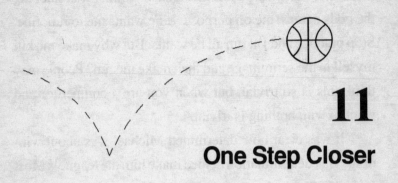

11
One Step Closer

Michael hated to lose. It still bothered him as much as it did when he was a teenager losing backyard games against his brother Larry.

During a scrimmage in training camp before the start of the 1987-88 NBA season, Michael stormed out of the gym before the scrimmage was over.

What happened?

"I'm a competitor, I want to win," Michael told reporters later that day. "I always keep score in everything. I know the score was 4-4. Coach Collins said it was 4-3 and my team was losing. After a long, tough practice, the losing

93

team has to run laps. I felt that Coach Collins was stacking the odds against me on purpose. If he wants me to run, fine. Stop practice and I'll run all he wants. But why make me kill myself in the scrimmage and then make me run? People may think this is so trivial, but when you are a competitor and want to win, nothing is trivial."

It was clear how determined Michael was about winning. That determination helped make him the league's Most Valuable Player that season. He also became the first player in NBA history to lead the league in scoring and steals during the same season. He was named the Defensive Player of the Year and the Most Valuable Player of the 1988 NBA All-Star Game.

Michael's determination also helped the Bulls become winners. They won 13 of their final 17 games and finished tied for second place with Atlanta in their division. For the first time since Michael had joined the Bulls in 1984, they had won more games than they had lost. The Bulls regular season record was 50 wins and 32 losses.

The Bulls also won in the playoffs that season. They played the Cleveland Cavaliers in the first round. Michael scored 50 points in the opening game of that series, leading the Bulls to a 104-93 victory.

It did not seem possible that Michael could play better than that, but he did. He scored 55 points in the second game, and the Bulls won, 106-101.

In the fourth quarter of Game 3, Michael tried for a layup and appeared to be fouled from both sides by bigger players. There seemed to be no way he could keep his balance and still score the basket. Somehow, he hung in the air, and he flipped the ball high off the backboard. It bounced down and into the basket! "The thing is, Michael doesn't get tired," said Ron Harper of the Cavaliers. "I get tired in the fourth quarter. Mike gets stronger."

As strong as Michael had been in that game, the Bulls lost 110-102. He scored 44 points in Game 4, but the Cavaliers won again, 97-91.

The playoff series was then decided by a fifth and final game. Michael really wanted to win that game. The Bulls had lost in the first round of the playoffs each year that Michael had played for them. He decided that they would do better this time.

At first, the game did not go well for the Bulls. They were behind, 39-29, only three minutes into the second quarter. Then Michael took over. He drove to the basket and scored four times in a row. Then he jumped up, caught a pass and dunked the ball. Suddenly, the Bulls were behind by only four points, 41-37.

Michael continued to pour it on. He finished the game with 39 points. The Bulls won 107-101. At last, they had won a playoff series!

The Bulls celebrated in their locker room after the game. They had beaten a good, young team, and Michael had set an NBA playoff record by scoring a total of 226 points in the five games. That total was nearly half of all the points the Bulls had scored together against the Cavaliers for the series. Even so, an important thing had happened. Michael had been helped by his teammates at important times.

One of those teammates was a rookie forward named Scottie Pippen, whom the Bulls had drafted out of Central Arkansas University the year before. When Michael went to the bench to rest late in the third quarter, Pippen stole a pass thrown by Ron Harper and scored. That basket gave the Bulls the lead for the first time in that game. Pippen then scored on a dunk. He later hit a jump shot that put the game out of reach.

"One-man team, huh?" asked Jerry Krause, the Bulls' general manager. "No way! No way this is a one-man team!"

That was good news for Michael. Even though the Bulls lost the next playoff series to the Detroit Pistons, they had taken an important step. They were becoming a team.

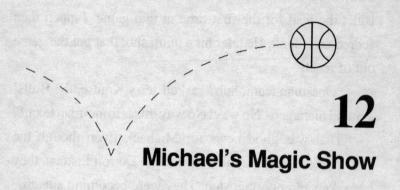

12

Michael's Magic Show

Michael and his teammates worked together in new ways during the 1988-89 season and produced some amazing results. Michael again led the NBA in scoring with a 32.5 points-per-game average. He recorded 15 "triple-doubles" during the season. A "triple-double" in basketball occurs when a player gets 10 or more points, rebounds and assists in one game.

Michael was able to do those things because he had switched from shooting guard to point guard at the end of that season in March. This allowed the Bulls to make better use of his passing, dribbling and rebounding skills.

Many players are not able to switch positions and play

well. Michael did it easily because he had followed his coach's advice when he was in college. "I really never thought I'd be a point guard, but Coach Smith used to tell me to work on my ball-handling," Michael says. "He said someday I may be playing point guard."

On January 25, 1989, Michael scored the 10,000th point of his NBA career in a game against the Philadelphia 76ers. It had taken him 303 games to score that many points. Only Wilt Chamberlain, who scored 10,000 points in his first 236 games, had reached that total faster.

It was a wonderful achievement for Michael, but he was disappointed. "I would rather have won the game," he said. The Bulls had lost 120-108.

The Bulls won 47 games and lost 35 that season. They finished fifth in their division. This was because they had lost eight of their last 11 games after Michael suffered a minor groin injury, Craig Hodges sprained his ankle, Horace Grant sprained his wrist and Scottie Pippen suffered an injury serious enough to slow him down. None of them stopped playing, though. They still made the playoffs.

Even though their record was not as good as it had been the year before, the Bulls were a better team. Michael's teammates had improved, and competitors could no longer concentrate only on Michael. If they did, the other Bulls could make good plays and score enough points to win the game.

Michael no longer had to do everything by himself. But there were times when he did and many of those times were in the playoffs.

The Bulls played the Cleveland Cavaliers again in the first round. The Cavaliers were even better than they had been the year before. They had won 57 games and lost only 25. They had also beaten the Bulls all six times that they had played them that season. Many sportswriters predicted that the Cavaliers would sweep the playoff series in three games.

Before that series began, the Bulls' players decided to wear black sneakers because Michael was. Players were not normally allowed to wear anything but white sneakers, but since Michael was wearing black ones, the rest of the team wore them so he would not be fined. They hoped that changing from white sneakers to black ones would bring them luck. It did. The Bulls won the first game, 95-88, on the Cavaliers' home court.

Nobody enjoyed winning that game more than

Michael. During the third quarter, he walked by the table where the sportswriters were sitting and made fun of their prediction. Michael had predicted that the Bulls would win the series in four games.

Cleveland won the second game, 96-88, even though Michael scored 30 points. Most players would be very happy to score 30 points in a playoff game against a good team like the Cavaliers. Michael was not. He thought he had played poorly.

Game 3 was played at Chicago Stadium. This time, even Coach Collins and the Bulls' cheerleaders wore lucky black sneakers. Michael then delighted the Bulls' fans by scoring 44 points to lead his team to a 101-94 victory. The Bulls needed to win one more game to take the playoff series.

Michael scored 50 points in Game 4. He played wonderfully, but when the game ended, Michael was unhappy. He had missed a free throw that would have given the Bulls a three-point lead with only nine seconds left to play in the game. His missed shot gave the Cavaliers a chance to tie the game, and they did. The game then went into overtime.

The Bulls then lost in a heartbreaker. They were behind, 107-105, with only 12 seconds left to play in overtime. Bill Cartwright tried to make a move to the basket, but Brad Daugherty of the Cavaliers stole the ball from him. Cleveland was fouled, hit the first basket and missed the second. The Bulls got the ball one last time, but the Cavs won, 108-105.

"I don't blame Bill," Michael said after the game. "I can't pin this loss on anyone but me."

The fifth, and final, game of the playoff series was held in Cleveland, Ohio. It was one of the most exciting games that Michael had played in since the 1982 college championship against Georgetown.

The Cavaliers held Michael to 14 points in the first half. But the Bulls stayed close, thanks to Bill Cartwright, who scored 12 points.

In the second half, Horace Grant, Scottie Pippen and Craig Hodges made big plays, while the Cavaliers continued to concentrate on stopping Michael. The Bulls had a 97-95 lead with only one minute and six seconds left to play in the game.

Craig Ehlo of the Cavaliers then sank a three-point shot to give his team the lead again. Michael came back with a jump shot that put the Bulls back on top, 99-98, but the game was not over.

Craig Ehlo of the Cavaliers scored on a layup to put Cleveland ahead, 100-99. There were only three seconds left to play. The Bulls called a timeout.

Coach Collins grabbed his chalkboard and sketched a play for his team. Every Bull knew who would get the ball in time to make one last shot. When the Bulls broke from their huddle, Michael whispered to Craig Hodges, "I'm going to make it."

Brad Sellers of the Bulls threw the ball inbounds from a spot at midcourt. Michael pretended that he was going to block a Cavalier player, then he ran to an open spot and caught Sellers' pass. Two Cavaliers ran at Michael. At the last second, he cut one way and they cut the other.

Michael was open in the middle of the court. He jumped up to shoot. Craig Ehlo of the Cavaliers closed in. Michael shot from just behind the free throw line . . . and scored! The Bulls had won!

"I never saw it go in, but I knew right away from the crowd reaction—silence—that it was good," Michael said. "I really celebrated. I was crushed after I missed that free throw in Game Four. I felt I had something to prove."

Michael proved himself again in the next playoff series. The Bulls' opponents were the New York Knicks, a strong team that had finished first in their division with a record of 52 wins and 30 losses. The Knicks were led by Patrick Ewing, the player who had given Michael and the Tar Heels such a tough time in the 1982 college championship game.

In a way, the Knicks and Bulls were similar to the Hoyas and the Tar Heels, and not only because the Knicks had Patrick Ewing and the Bulls had Michael Jordan. The Knicks were a strong defensive team, as the Hoyas had been. They used a tactic called the "press" in which each Knick covered an opposing player so closely that he had little room to dribble or shoot—and little time to pass.

The Bulls were like the Tar Heels. They relied on quickness and ability to shoot, especially Michael's.

The Knicks were predicted to win the series. The first game was played in New York City at Madison Square Garden, where the Knicks had lost only six games all season.

The Bulls surprised the Knicks and their fans by playing the Knicks' own tough style of defense. The Knicks led, 103-95, with just under four minutes left to play in the game, but the Bulls kept them from scoring another basket during regulation time. They tied the score, 103-103, and the game went into overtime. Then Michael got going. He scored 10 of the 34 points he got in the game to give the Bulls a 120-109 victory.

In Game 2, it was the Knicks' turn to play tough defense. They held Michael to only 15 points, and won, 114-97. It was a convincing victory, but the Knicks had made a serious mistake that came back to haunt them. It happened when Mark Jackson of the Knicks made fun of Michael by sticking his tongue out as he dribbled downcourt. Xavier McDaniel could have told Jackson what happens when you make Michael Jordan mad.

Jackson found out in Game 3, at Chicago Stadium. Michael scored 40 points, grabbed 15 rebounds, got 9 assists and made 6 steals. He drove the Knicks crazy by scooting around them when they tried to use their press. When they tried to block his path to the basket, Michael sank jump shots.

The Bulls won the game by 23 points, 111-88. Even though Michael had suffered a groin injury in the first half, he had done everything except stuff the Knicks into their gym bags and send them back to New York.

Michael's injury bothered him in Game 4. He ran with a limp, but it didn't matter. The Bulls won again, 106-93. Michael scored 47 points, grabbed 11 rebounds, got 6 assists and blocked 2 shots. He broke the game open when he scored 18 points in the fourth quarter, even though his injury had become very sore.

"Once I got out there, I wasn't going to think of myself as being hurt," Michael said. "This is a playoff game."

The Bulls needed to win only one more game to eliminate the Knicks from the playoffs. They knew it would not be easy. The Knicks were desperate, and Game 5 would be played on their home court. Michael scored 38 points in that game, but the Bulls could not stop Patrick Ewing the way they had done in the first four games. Ewing broke loose and scored 32 points, as the Knicks won 121-114.

The Bulls still had a big advantage because Game 6 would be played at Chicago Stadium. The crowd of 18,676 fans roared from the opening jump ball to the final minute. Michael scored 40 points, and the Bulls held Ewing to 22, but the game went down to the wire.

The score was tied, and there were only four seconds

left to play in the game, when Michael stepped to the free throw line. The crowd knew victory was at hand. The Knicks knew they were doomed. "In that situation, with that time on the clock, you're talking about Superman," said Rick Pitino, the Knicks' coach. "He's the best player who ever lived."

Michael made both free throws to give the Bulls a 113-111 win. Chicago Stadium exploded. The Bulls had upset the mighty Knicks in the playoffs!

It was a sweet victory, and an important one, because Michael's teammates had given him help when he needed it. In those six games, Scottie Pippen and Bill Cartwright both had scoring averages of more than 14 points per game. Cartwright had also rebounded well, and had done a fine job defending against Patrick Ewing.

The Bulls' next playoff opponents were the tough Detroit Pistons, who had the best record in the NBA that season. The team that won the series would then play in the final round for the NBA Championship.

Few people thought that the Bulls could win even one playoff game against the Pistons, who had defeated them the last six times they had played. The Pistons had won 63 games and lost only 19 that season, and their defense was very, very tough. The Pistons were known as "The Bad Boys" because they played a very physical game and liked to knock opposing players down.

People were shocked when Michael told reporters, "We win the first game, we win the series. Write that down. Remember what I said."

Usually, when a player makes a bold prediction like Michael did, he sounds arrogant and makes the other team angry. "Michael's never done anything in an arrogant way," said Coach Collins. "He's just like the old Western gunslinger. Every time he walks out, he's got to prove he is the quickest gun in the West."

Michael really wanted to prove that the people who said his team could not win were wrong. "We can win this series," he said. "I'm not going to lay down and let the Pistons walk all over me."

In Game 1, the Bulls surprised the Pistons by taking a 14-4 lead midway through the first quarter. By the middle of the second quarter, the Bulls led, 46-22. The Pistons were confused and disorganized. The Bulls' defense allowed Detroit's best scorer, Isiah Thomas, to score on only 3 of his

18 shots during the entire game.

The Pistons got themselves together during halftime, and they started a ferocious attack. They shut down Michael's ability to score, and wore down the Bulls' defense. Chicago's big lead began to shrink.

The Bulls were so tired by the fourth quarter that they could barely fight for rebounds. In the last 15 minutes of the game, the Pistons scored 17 points after grabbing the rebounds off their own shots. Luckily, Scottie Pippen came to the rescue. He grabbed five rebounds in the fourth quarter to help the Bulls hold off the Pistons. The Bulls won, 94-88, with 32 points scored by Michael.

The Pistons were stunned that they had lost. Fans and sportswriters were amazed. Even Coach Collins was surprised. "Yes, I'm really surprised, and you are, too," he told reporters after the game. "So, we're all surprised together. We can all have a surprise party."

Actually, Michael had known all along that the Bulls would win. "I had a good feeling about this game," he said. "I told my teammates before the game that the pressure was not on us. We've gone further in the playoffs than anybody thought we would, so let's catch the Pistons on their heels today because it will be really hard to do it later."

Michael was right. The Pistons defense held Michael to 27 points in Game 2, and Detroit won, 100-91. The Bulls were in for the fight of their lives.

Game 3 brought out the best in Michael, who put on an amazing show. The Bulls were losing, 90-77, with only 6 minutes and 17 seconds left to play in the game, when Michael exploded to score 12 points.

He floated through the Pistons defense and scored on a layup. He sank a 16-foot and a 12-foot jump shot. The first one cut the Pistons' lead to 95-91, with only 1:55 seconds left to play. Horace Grant later tied the game at 97-97 by sinking two free throws. There were only 28 seconds left on the clock.

The Bulls got a big break when Bill Laimbeer of the Pistons committed an offensive foul with only nine seconds left. The ball was then given to the Bulls. "I knew we were in trouble then," said Chuck Daly, Detroit's coach.

On the next play, the Bulls got the ball to Michael. There were three seconds left when he launched an eight-foot shot while he was still running to the basket. The shot was good! The Bulls had won, 99-97.

"Thank God for Michael," said Craig Hodges.

Michael had scored a total of 46 points and grabbed 7 rebounds. He also had five steals and five assists. Many people were speechless over the way he had brought the Bulls to victory after they had been so far behind.

"Words cannot explain Michael Jordan," said Charles Davis of the Bulls. "If you look in Latin, or some other language, and find a word to do it, let me know. I'm just glad I'm on his side."

That game was the last one the Bulls would win in the playoffs. Michael's magic show woke the Pistons up, and they got rough in Game 4 and won, 86-80. Michael scored 23 points.

In Game 5, the Pistons pounded Michael and held him to only 18 points. Detroit won, 94-85. Michael fought back gallantly in Game 6 and scored 32 points, but the Pistons won the game, 103-94, and the series. The Bulls' season was over.

Naturally, Michael was disappointed. However, losing to the Pistons was nothing to be ashamed of, as Detroit went on to sweep the Los Angeles Lakers in four games to win the NBA Championship.

Michael and the Bulls had every reason to feel proud. They had beaten teams when people thought they would lose. They had gone farther in the playoffs than ever before. Michael had set an NBA playoff record by scoring an average of 34.8 points per game in the 17 postseason games he had played. He had also scored 40 or more points in seven of those games.

Of all those accomplishments, Michael says his best moment in the playoffs that year was the shot he made against the Cavaliers that won the first series for the Bulls. "That was the highlight of everything," he says. "It was something that a lot of people said could not be done, and yet we believed in ourselves and we did it."

Coach Collins was very proud of Michael and his teammates because of all they had accomplished. "The thing I'm so delighted about now is that Michael was always being written about as an individual player," he said. "It does my heart good because he now has a team that can let him show what he is all about."

13

The Dream Season

Losing is sometimes the best way to learn how to win. A good team often becomes a great team after it suffers a tough defeat in a big game or a playoff. The disappointment teaches players to be more determined and to work harder together. They learn what it takes to be champions.

Michael and his teammates learned a painful but valuable lesson during the 1989-90 season. Their record of 55-27 was Chicago's best since 1971-72. Michael won the NBA scoring title again with a 33.6 points-per-game average. Scottie Pippen became an All-Star for the first time.

In the playoffs, the Bulls defeated the Bucks three games to one in the first round and crushed the 76ers four games to one in the second. But in the Eastern Conference Finals, the Bulls were beaten by the Pistons in a hard-fought seven-game series.

Losing to Detroit was very frustrating for the Bulls. It was the third straight year that they had been beaten by the Pistons in the playoffs. The loss was especially bitter for Michael, who saw his dream of winning a championship dashed once again.

Michael was also stung by criticism from fans and sportswriters. They questioned his greatness as a player by pointing to his failure to lead the Bulls to an NBA title.

Many people believe that the ability to lead a team to a championship is the real mark of greatness. Magic Johnson had led the Lakers to five NBA titles. Larry Bird had led the Celtics to three. Michael had won four scoring titles and an MVP award, but people were beginning to say he wasn't a good leader or the kind of player who makes his teammates better.

Magic Johnson, for example, used his dazzling passing skills to make his teammates become important parts of the Lakers' offense. Larry Bird led the Celtics by setting an example on the court and then pushing his teammates to practice and play as hard as he did.

As for Michael, he was still the one the Bulls counted on whenever games were on the line, particularly playoff games. His teammates, especially Scottie Pippen, John Paxson and Horace Grant, *had* improved. They just hadn't done enough to step out of Michael's shadow. People still thought of them as Michael's "supporting cast" and called them "The Jordanaires" and "The Jordanaries," as a play on the word "ordinary."

After the playoff loss to the Pistons, Michael became more determined than ever to reach his dream and prove his critics wrong. He was convinced that he and his teammates had to work together as never before if they wanted to reach the top.

When Michael got to training camp in the fall of 1990, he began pushing his teammates to accept more responsibility for the team's success.

"I'm looking now at a division title and a world title," he told reporters. "My challenge is not my individual play but this team and what we want to achieve. That means I have to do my job on the court, and I've got to push the other guys to have the same determination I have. That's the only way we're going to win."

Phil Jackson, who became the Bulls' head coach before the 1989-90 season, agreed. He knew the Bulls depended too often on Michael. In the previous four seasons, Michael had scored nearly one third of the team's total points. Some of that load had to be taken off Michael's shoulders.

Coach Jackson decided to use an offense that required all the players to get more involved. This new offense used a lot of running and passing. The plan was to get the ball to the open player who had the easiest shot, instead of constantly passing to Michael and counting on him to use his wizardry to get to the basket.

Michael was expected to make fewer flying dunks. Instead, he would play closer to the basket, where he would try for easy layups and short jump shots. If he was covered too closely, he would pass. It was possible that Michael would end up passing more and scoring less. People wondered if he could accept playing in an offense that might prevent him from winning the scoring title.

"It limits him, no doubt about it," Coach Jackson told

reporters. "But we've let Michael try to win by himself and we've come up short. So let's see if we can get other people involved. It's not like we're saying that Michael absolutely *cannot* win the scoring title. I told him it would hurt his scoring. But I told him, 'You will still score anyway, and it will help the team.'"

Michael was happy to do whatever he was asked. He lifted weights to make himself stronger. This made it harder for opponents to push him away from the basket. He worked on improving his passing skills.

When the 1990-91 season began, the Bulls struggled and lost their first 3 games and 6 of their first 11. Their new offense was complicated and hard to learn. The players, Michael included, often looked confused. They needed time to become familiar with a lot of new plays.

It took about three weeks before the Bulls felt comfortable with the new offense. Then they went on a seven-game winning streak. By the end of December, they had lost only 3 times in their last 18 games.

The holiday season was a very merry one for Michael. Not only were the Bulls doing well, but on Christmas Eve day, his wife, Juanita, gave birth to their second son, Marcus

James Jordan. The next night, Michael celebrated by scoring 37 points as the Bulls beat the Pistons, 98-86.

"It was very inspiring to go out and play knowing that you've helped bring somebody into the world," Michael said after the game. "I figured the only way it would get better is if we went out and beat up on the Pistons. Then we did."

It kept getting better. When the Bulls paused for All-Star Weekend in February, they had a 32-14 record and were behind the first-place Pistons by only one and a half games. Michael played in the All-Star Game and was the leading scorer with 26 points as the East beat the West, 116-114.

Then it was back to business. The Bulls caught fire and won 19 of their next 21 games to claim the best record in the NBA (51-16). They were working together beautifully. They were almost unstoppable on offense and sparkling on defense. They had won 36 games by 10 points or more and 6 by 30 or more!

As expected, Michael's scoring average (30.8 points per game) was lower than it had been the previous season (33.6), but he was still leading the league. There were nights when he exploded for 35 or 40 points. More often, he spent the first half of games helping his teammates do most of the scoring. If the score was still close or if the Bulls were losing in the second half, then he would come to the rescue.

Fortunately, the Bulls didn't have to call on Michael too often. Scottie Pippen's scoring average (17.2 points) was the best of his career, and he had improved his rebounding (7.2) and assist averages (6.1) as well. John Paxson and Horace Grant were among the league leaders in field goal percentage.

"In terms of a team concept, this is, by far, the best of all my years with the team," Michael said. "Everyone's contributing. Yes, we still have a lot to prove. Don't think we've achieved what Detroit has. They've won two world championships, and we haven't won any. We're trying to get where they are. And we think we can."

In their final game of the regular season, the Bulls beat Detroit, 108-100. Chicago's 61-21 record was the best in the team's history. Michael won his fifth consecutive scoring title (31.5), but it meant very little to him. The playoffs were next, and the only thing that mattered was winning the championship.

The Bulls played like demons in the first two rounds. They swept the Knicks in three games and blew away the

76ers in five. Then came the biggest challenge Michael and his teammates had ever faced: a matchup against their fiercest rivals, the Pistons.

The Pistons were trying to win their third consecutive NBA championship. They were called "The Bad Boys" because of their extremely rough, physical style of play. In past playoffs, they had beaten the Bulls by bullying and intimidating them. This time, the Bulls were intent on giving the Pistons a taste of their own medicine.

Seventy seconds into Game 1 in Chicago, Michael rapped Pistons guard Joe Dumars in the chest with a forearm and sent him reeling. Seven minutes later, Michael drew a foul for elbowing Dennis Rodman. Then, with only 38 seconds left in the first half, Michael yelled at Rodman, "You can't stop me!"

Michael almost stopped himself with his shenanigans. He scored only 22 points in the game, but his teammates came through. The Bulls shocked the Pistons with their hard-nosed play and won, 94-83.

The next day, Michael attended a news conference where he received the NBA's MVP award. He graciously accepted the trophy and thanked his teammates for their support during the season. Then he made it clear that something more important was on his mind.

"Winning the MVP Award is great," he told reporters. "But I'd much rather be standing here in June, waiting to receive a championship ring."

In Game 2, the Bulls' defense hounded the Pistons into making turnovers and bad shots. Michael did not score his first basket until there were only two minutes and 18 seconds left in the first period, but Scottie Pippen scored 16 points to help the Bulls take a 49-41 lead at the half.

In the second half, Michael erupted for 27 of his 35 points, and the Bulls never let Detroit get closer than six points. Chicago drew away for an easy 105-97 win.

"This feels good," Michael said after the game. "We've put them in a tough position. We're confident we can beat this team."

The Pistons had other ideas. The series was moving to their home court, and they weren't going to give up without a fight. "We play an intense style, and it's going to be even more intense on Saturday," Pistons forward John Salley warned. "Maybe one of the most intense games you've ever seen."

Unfortunately for the Pistons, the Bulls put that intensity to better use in Game 3 and jumped out to a 24-8 lead. In one electrifying sequence early in the game, Scottie Pippen and John Paxson trapped Pistons guard Isiah Thomas in the backcourt. They forced him to pass to forward James Edwards. Michael ran right at Edwards and nearly jumped over him while batting the ball away. Paxson recovered the ball and sank a jump shot.

The Pistons grew frustrated, and it showed. Detroit forward Mark Aguirre punched the ball out of Horace Grant's hands during a time-out in the first period. Less than a minute later, Aguirre shoved Grant and was called for a technical foul. Later, with 50 seconds left to play in the game, Dennis Rodman slammed the ball into Michael's stomach and was called for a technical. While the Pistons were unraveling, Michael stayed cool. In the final period, he scored 14 of his 33 points to seal a 113-107 win. "We made them crumble, made them scramble, made them come apart," Michael said after the game. "That's always what they've done to us in the past."

Two days later, the Bulls eliminated the Pistons in a 115-94 blowout. As time was running out, the players on the

Pistons' bench walked silently past the Bulls' bench and into the locker room. They didn't stop for the customary post-game handshake between teams. It was a terrible display of poor sportsmanship, but it didn't take away from the joy Michael and his teammates were feeling. They were going to the championship finals to face the Lakers!

The NBA finals were a dream matchup featuring the league's two most popular players. Fans had long debated who was better, Magic Johnson or Michael Jordan, and now they would find out.

Game 1 was played in Chicago before a screaming crowd of 18,676. The contest was intense and incredibly dramatic throughout. Neither team led by more than seven points at any time. The lead changed hands 24 times. There was a wild ending.

The Bulls were ahead 91-89 with 35 seconds left in the game when Michael missed a 12-foot shot. Then, with 14 seconds left, Magic Johnson whipped a cross-court pass to Sam Perkins, Michael's former college teammate. As Horace Grant flew at Perkins, Perkins set himself and lofted a 26-foot shot that was good for three points. The Lakers led 92-91.

The Bulls had one last chance, and the crowd was on its feet. Scottie Pippen passed to Michael, who was about 18 feet from the basket. Michael made a stop-and-go move to get by Sam Perkins and launched a 15-foot jump shot. The ball went about one-third of the way into the basket and then spun back out. The rebound went to Lakers guard Byron Scott, who was then fouled and made one of two free throws.

The game ended with Scottie Pippen heaving a desperate 60-foot shot that clanged off the back rim. The joyous, victorious Lakers celebrated their 93-91 win.

Michael didn't dwell on his missed shot or the defeat. As the Bulls' leader, he knew he had to rally his teammates. He had scored 36 points in the game, but some of the other Bulls had played poorly. John Paxson, for example, had made only three of his seven shots. So before Game 2, Michael told him, "If we go down, we have to go down with no bullets in our holster. So shoot."

The Bulls came out shooting, and they rose to Michael's challenge by setting a playoff record for accuracy (61.7 percent). John Paxson sank all 8 of his shots. Horace

Grant hit 10 of 13. Bill Cartwright hit 6 of 9. Scottie Pippen sank 8 of his 16 field goals and made all 4 of his free throws.

In the early going, Michael passed constantly and wound up with 13 assists. He didn't start shooting until after the Bulls opened a seven-point halftime lead. By the end of the third quarter, he had sunk 13 consecutive shots and ended up scoring 33 points. The Bulls won easily, 107-86.

That victory turned the tide of the championship series in the Bulls' favor. They began swamping the Lakers with an awesome display of teamwork.

In Game 3 in Los Angeles, the Lakers led 67-54 in the third period before eight different Bulls scored to tie the game at 74-74 midway through the fourth period. Chicago then won in overtime, 104-96.

In Game 4, Michael dished out 13 assists as Scottie Pippen, Horace Grant, John Paxson and Bill Cartwright contributed greatly to Chicago's 97-82 win.

"They are beating us, and beating us bad," Magic Johnson said after the game. "When Michael gets going great, and the rest of them are going great, they're unbeatable. I tip my hat to my competitor. He's doing a great job."

So were the rest of the Bulls. They were proving they weren't "Jordanaries" after all. They were a championship basketball team. "We all realize that Michael is the greatest player in the world, but we also know that we all have a part in all of this," John Paxson said.

"Michael is so exceptional because he gets everyone else involved," said Bulls assistant coach Jim Cleamons. "He had to learn all that. All teamwork does is win games. You can't be selfish and win a championship."

Michael stood on the threshold of his dream. All that was needed was one more victory. "I'm nervous," he told reporters at practice before Game 5. "It's tough to control my emotions. Every now and then I get chill bumps thinking about the situation. I want it for myself as well as the team so we can celebrate together."

The Bulls indeed looked nervous on their big night. Scottie Pippen made only two of his first nine shots and committed five turnovers. Michael even missed several easy shots and committed four turnovers. Chicago went into the locker room down 49-48 at the half.

The Bulls settled down during halftime. Then they

opened a 70-62 lead midway through the fourth period with Scottie Pippen dunking majestically and scoring 12 of his 32 points. Pippen, not Michael, ended up as the Bulls' leading scorer that night as Chicago wrapped up the championship with a 108-101 win.

Michael, who scored 30 points, was unanimously chosen as Playoff MVP. "I could care less," he said. "The whole team is the MVP."

As Michael left the court, a camera crew began shooting him for an "I'm Going to Disney World!" commercial. Michael insisted that Scottie Pippen, Horace Grant, John Paxson and Bill Cartwright be included, too.

In the locker room, Michael cried tears of joy as Juanita and his dad stood by. He had almost stopped crying when a friend led a smiling woman into the room. It was Michael's mother. Michael broke down again as his mom kissed him and patted him on the cheek.

"I've never been this emotional in public, but I don't mind," Michael said. "I don't know if I'll ever have this feeling again. All the struggles, all the people saying, 'He's not gonna win,' all those little doubts you have about yourself. You have to put them aside and think positive. I am gonna win! I am a winner! And then when you do it, well, it's just amazing."

The Bulls celebrated that night at a party in Los Angeles. When Michael got home to Chicago the next afternoon, about 100 friends and neighbors were waiting. There were letters of congratulations and a telegram from Coach Dean Smith of the University of North Carolina. Balloons, posters and drawings were tacked to Michael's front door. Plants and bouquets of flowers were everywhere. The next day, the city of Chicago honored the Bulls with a rally and motorcade.

After all the celebrations quieted down, Michael was asked by a reporter from *Sports Illustrated* how he felt now that his dream had come true.

"The difference is in here," he said, tapping his chest. "I think people will now feel it's O.K. to put me in the category of players like Magic. The championship, in the minds of a lot of people, is a sign of, well, greatness. I guess they can say that about me now."

BASKETBALL COURT

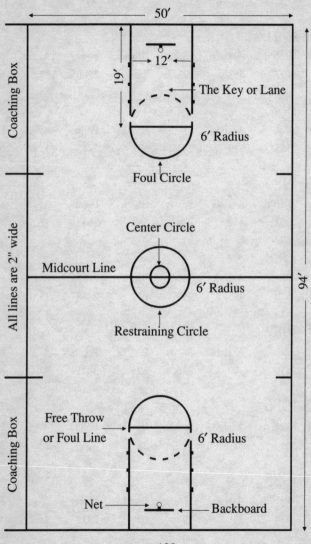

50′

Coaching Box

19′

12′

The Key or Lane

6′ Radius

Foul Circle

All lines are 2″ wide

Center Circle

Midcourt Line

6′ Radius

Restraining Circle

94′

Coaching Box

Free Throw or Foul Line

6′ Radius

Net

Backboard

Michael's NBA Statistics

1990-1991

Games	Reb'ds.	Assists	Steals	Blocks	Points	Avg.	High
82	492	453	223	83	2580	31.5	46

1989-1990

Games	Reb'ds.	Assists	Steals	Blocks	Points	Avg.	High
82	565	519	241	54	2753	33.6	69

1988-1989

Games	Reb'ds.	Assists	Steals	Blocks	Points	Avg.	High
81	652	650	234	65	2633	32.5	53

1987-1988

Games	Reb'ds.	Assists	Steals	Blocks	Points	Avg.	High
82	449	485	259	131	2868	35.0	59

1986-1987

Games	Reb'ds.	Assists	Steals	Blocks	Points	Avg.	High
82	430	377	236	125	3041	37.1	61

1985-1986

Games	Reb'ds.	Assists	Steals	Blocks	Points	Avg.	High
18	64	53	37	21	408	22.7	33

1984-1985

Games	Reb'ds.	Assists	Steals	Blocks	Points	Avg.	High
82	534	481	196	69	2313	28.2	49